In Good Faith
The Strong Negotiation of President Eisenhower

In Good Faith:
   The Strong Negotiation of President Eisenhower
Copyright © 2022 Dr. Lou Villaire
Anchor Book Press
440 W Colfax Street, Unit 1132, Palatine, IL 60078
ISBN: 9781949109832
Library of Congress Control Number: 2021950073
Printed in the United States

All rights reserved. No part of this publication may be reproduced, stored in a retrieval system, or transmitted in any form by any means – electronic, mechanical, photocopy, recording, or any other – except for brief quotations, without the prior written permission of the author.

In Good Faith
The Strong Negotiation of President Eisenhower

Dr. Lou Villaire
ANCHOR BOOK PRESS • Palatine

Table of Contents

Preface 1

Introduction 3

Chapter 1 7
President Eisenhower: The Strongest American Negotiator

Chapter 2 23
The 20th Century Korean Armistice: Know When to Call a Fight

Chapter 3 59
The Suez Crisis of 1956: Leverage What You Have

Chapter 4 87
The Civil Rights Act of 1957: Negotiate with Conscience and Guile

Chapter 5 121
The Steel Strike of 1959: Be an Honest Broker with Your Self Interest

Chapter 6: 145
The U2 Incident of 1960: Count to Ten Before You Say Anything

Chapter 7 181
Eisenhower and the Middle Way of Strong Negotiation

Afterward 195

Index 215

About the Author 233

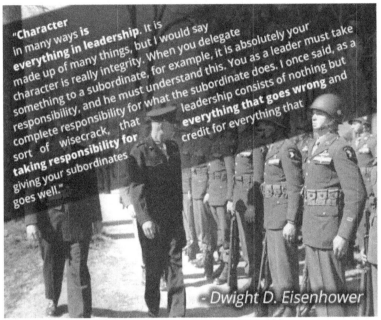

Figure 1: Puryear, Jr. 1971, 1992, 289

"*Suaviter in Modo, Fortier in Re*"
"Gentle in Manner, Strong in Deed"
Claudio Acquaviva

Desk plaque Given to Eisenhower by Gabriel Hauge,
Assistant to the President for Economic Affairs from 1953 to 1958.

In Good Faith

Preface

"*Suaviter in Modo, Fortier in Re*" "Gentle in Manner, Strong in Deed" (Claudio Acquaviva 1543-1615) is the inscription on a paperweight that Dwight David Eisenhower kept on his desk in the Oval Office of the White House. This maxim was a guide to remind him how to conduct his affairs. This quote is a guide, especially in those activities which require us to negotiate with others - which is a great deal of what we do every day.

In Good Faith is a book of history, a self-help history book about one of the most consequential presidents in US history. The purpose of this book is to help the reader improve negotiating skills through the stories that illustrate the skills and strategies used by the most successful American negotiator - President Dwight David Eisenhower.

The historical events told in this book are major national and international events of the last century (1950-1960). These events determined the character of our nation and the political realities of our world. President Eisenhower is the main character in these events during his eight years as the 34th president.

Researching and writing this book has challenged the author to understand how and why these events changed our nation and our world. How an extraordinary man from ordinary origins shaped events with his skill as a statesman and a negotiator, as well as a man who was often quick to temper. The outcomes of the events were also influenced by the mistakes that Eisenhower made, his misperceptions, and even some of his irritable bullying. Yet, in the eight years of the Ike Presidency, zero American lives were lost in international conflicts of his making. This is a testament to the negotiation and diplomacy skills of Eisenhower. Ike had a commitment to peaceful solutions to international and domestic conflicts.

Ike influenced and shaped our nation in the middle half of the 20th century more than any other individual. From the post-WWII *Pax Americana*, the North Atlantic Treaty Organization (NATO), the Cold War, to the unprecedented expansion of the interdependent world economy. Ike was a great advocate of free trade. Ike understood and insisted that robust international trade is ultimately a greater deterrent to conflict than any number of armaments.

Many books have been written about Eisenhower the man, the leader, the soldier, and the United States president. This book biographies Eisenhower as a political leader, a negotiator. Colleagues of Ike were asked about essential qualities that Ike possessed. They reported that Ike's most important quality was his ability to 'bring people together' - people of differing views and differing vested interests. Ultimate success, whether you are the leader of a local citizen group, or the leader of the free world depends on strong negotiation skills. Strong negotiation is the ability 'to give and to take,' to clearly think through outcomes, be tough-minded, and lead with integrity.

Introduction

All day, every day, we negotiate to get what we want. To get more of what we want, we must be strong negotiators. Strong negotiation gives us greater power in our lives. Strong negotiating gets us a better job with higher pay, a happier and more harmonious home life, and the respect and regard of our community. Negotiating with strength is a path to power and success. Our strength as negotiators comes from practiced negotiation skills and our integrity as individuals.

President Dwight David Eisenhower is commemorated as the Supreme Commander of Allied Forces during WWII and as a successful two-term US president from 1953-1960. The Eisenhower administration is remembered for the US Interstate Highway System, integration of US public schools (Brown vs. Board of Education, 1954) and presiding over a post-WWII US industrial economic expansion. Eisenhower was one of the world's most successful leaders with upstanding moral credibility. The most essential skill that Eisenhower learned and practiced was strong negotiation. Eisenhower *became a great leader by being a great negotiator.*

While Eisenhower had strong moral authority as a negotiator, he was neither sanctimonious nor homespun, as he is often portrayed. Eisenhower could be deceptive when necessary. For example, Eisenhower was often cunning with the press, playing the part of the bumbling elder statesman. Eisenhower was far from a righteous man - he could obfuscate, dissemble, and misdirect. Eisenhower failed to do what was right sometimes, but he almost always acted in good faith.

Lou Villaire

Negotiation is a skill like hunting, playing the piano, or teaching. As with most skills, negotiation can be learned with proper training and practice. This book conveys stories, and from these stories the reader gains knowledge of the skills needed to be a strong negotiator. The lessons learned come from pictures of 20th Century US history where Eisenhower used his skills as a strong negotiator to reach a desired outcome.

Strong negotiators share certain qualities. One prominent quality is a deep desire to understand human history. Strong negotiators learn from the past rather than nurturing a view of how events should be. For the strong negotiator, history is empirical. This book takes you through five stories of powerful negotiation by Eisenhower. There are numerous examples of strategies, tactics, and actions used by Eisenhower as a strong negotiator. Eisenhower demonstrates the basic qualities of a strong negotiator. He teaches us to act 'in good faith' with personal integrity, giving ourselves power and strength. Eisenhower shows us how to apply force when we need force.

In the context of Korean history and the Korean War, Eisenhower negotiated the very contentious Korean Armistice. Eisenhower understood that there are conflicts and negotiations, in which the best you can accomplish is a long-term, uneasy truce. Eisenhower knew the Korean War was a lose/lose situation, and he successfully extracted the United States from Korea.

In the Mid-East Suez Canal Crisis, Eisenhower used his negotiating power to change the outcome and get what he wanted. In this crisis, Eisenhower was misled by US allies. However, his swift and strong actions established a longstanding and muscular US presence in the Mid-East. A highly visible US presence that remains to this day.

The Civil Rights Act of 1957 was the first US civil rights legislation since the US Civil War Reconstruction. Here Eisenhower used his principled authority and the ambitions of a US congressman (who later became a US president) to pass civil rights legislation that was opposed by powerful segregationist, Southern senators.

In 1959, the US economy had a near shutdown as a result of the nationwide steel strike. Eisenhower used his skills (and the self-interests of others) as an honest broker in that conflict. This US labor strike lasted 116 days. The US steel industry failed to recover from this strike.

Figure 2: June 7, 1944, English Channel, Eisenhower Library

Eisenhower lied to the world about the 1960 U2 plane incident. We learn how Eisenhower eventually confessed his deception and how he negotiated away from the conflict, but with lasting damage to international relations.

We can put the lessons from this book into practice in our own lives and become stronger negotiators and more powerful people, getting more of what we want from life.

This book follows several extraordinary events in chronological order during the Eisenhower presidency from 1952 through 1960, with the election of John F. Kennedy as the US president. Ike is accompanied in these stories by several commanding United States and world leaders, including the populist president of Egypt, Gamal Abdel Nasser, Lyndon Baines Johnson, Nikita Khrushchev, Syngman Rhee, the president of South Korea, and the leaders of one of the largest industries in the world, the US steelworkers, and the US steel corporations.

Chapter 1
President Eisenhower: The Strongest American Negotiator

Ike's longtime press secretary and close confidant James 'Jim' Haggerty was asked what he thought was Ike's greatest accomplishment. Tom Wicker reports Hagerty's response, "Getting people to compromise divergent views without anyone's surrender of principles" (2002, p. 138).

The eight years of the Eisenhower presidency from 1953-1960 are known for postwar economic growth and a number of perilous world events. Eisenhower dealt with several major crises, including the Korean War, a crisis in the Mid-East, and escalating military tensions between the United States and the Soviet Union. At home, Eisenhower was confronted with the civil rights movement and labor unrest. Ike and his trusted advisors negotiated all of these international and domestic perils with cold conscience and resilience.

Despite all of these international and domestic threats, Eisenhower's presidency included some of the most prosperous years in the history of the United States. Real change in US GDP under Ike increased over 20%. The real median income for Americans rose 20%. US debt as a percentage of GDP dropped 20%. The US stock market increased 150%, and US job growth increased 5% a year. Eisenhower continued many New Deal programs, expanded Social Security, and prioritized a balanced budget over tax cuts (Wicker, 2020). Why was Ike a *strong negotiator*? Ike had lessons from a young age.

Ike liked to tell a story of when he was a little boy at his uncle's farm. There was a gander who would repeatedly attack young Ike. "My enemy was a bad-tempered and aggressive gander. I was a little boy, not yet five years old, who was intensely curious about the new environment into which he was thrust and determined to explore its every corner. But the gander constantly balked at me. He obviously looked upon me as a harmless and helpless nuisance. He had no intention of permitting anyone to penetrate his domain. Always hopeful that he would finally abandon his threatened attacks on my person, I'd try again and again, always with the same result" (Eisenhower, 1967, p. 50).

Ike's Uncle Luther finally decided something had to be done. So Uncle Luther took an old broom and cut off all of the straw except for a short, hard knob. Uncle Luther then took little Ike into the yard and showed him how to swing at the gander to keep the bird away. Next time the gander went after Ike, Ike wielded the broom and smacked the gander on the backside. The gander squawked and ran off. Thereafter, Ike said, he would brandish the broom when the gander became aggressive. He kept his distance, and "I was the proud boss of the back yard. This all turned out to be a rather good lesson for me because I quickly learned never to negotiate with an adversary except from a position of strength" (Eisenhower, 1967, p. 50).

General Goodpaster (Ike's staff secretary and later NATO commander) once described Ike's grasp of human behavior in the context of card games, "Ike was a consummate bridge player. He's a great poker player, and an extremely good bridge player. He plays bridge very much in poker style and he's a tremendous man for analyzing the other fellow's mind. Which options are open to the other fellow, and what line he can best take to capitalize or exploit the possibilities, having figured the options open to the other man" (Thomas, 2012, page 195).

Ike was an accomplished bridge player, bridge being a game of skill, logic, and psychology. According to Fred Greenstein in his 1982 book, *The Hidden Hand Presidency*, what Ike liked about bridge was the time it gave him to drive for the solution to an analytical problem while mastering the psychology of cooperating with his partner and competing with his opponents (p. 195).

Ike was often impatient with people, especially if he thought that they were belaboring a point. Ike's impatience was a strength and a weakness. His impatience was a strength inasmuch as Ike had a unique and compulsory intelligence. Ike had a rapid wit. He was clear-sighted and perceptive with relentless nervous energy to drive issues forward and to solve hard problems. Ike's cabinet members told stories of how Ike would listen to a speaker at a cabinet meeting while Ike tapped his pencil on his thigh. And if Ike thought you were putting too fine a point on your message, he would cut you short and move on to the next topic.

When Ike got angry, his face would become a pale red, and his clear blue eyes would become steel blue. Ike's anger was usually fleeting. One of his aides described Ike's anger as a quick passing storm. Ike had a habit of looking people up and down silently, studying them, and then acknowledging them with an uneasy OK.

Ike would discontinue relationships with individuals if the relationship was unrequired. According to Fred Greenstein, if Ike recognized someone as having grave character defects, absent any compelling reason to deal with him, Ike would stop any association with that individual (1994). Unfortunately, in many negotiations, we rarely have that luxury; we must deal with our counterpart in the best way that we are able.

Ike avoided subtleties of personalities. He parsimoniously identified principal traits of persons. Ike had a term for his character summaries of individuals as *personal equations*. "What is his personal equation?" Ike would ask about a man. "Who is he?" This was an extraordinary reduction of the complex character of most persons. Yet, it allowed Ike to engage with an incredible number of individuals.

Ike also understood the power of optimism in persuasion and success. The historian, Steven Ambrose, claimed that Ike believed that to attain victory, the negotiator must display confidence, enthusiasm, and optimism in the command. Ambrose writes that Ike showed confidence and support even when he felt otherwise (1990).

In the course of various negotiations, Ike knew personal feelings had to be subordinate to the duties of leadership. Uncontrolled displays of anger in a negotiation weaken your strength. Ike said in a CBS interview, "I learned a long time ago that anybody that aspired to a position of leadership of any kind, must learn to control his temper" (Columbia Broadcasting System, 1964). Ike understood his own inclination to anger and factored it into his own personal equation and his own leadership. Ike's notorious temper was also a byproduct of his perpetual state of nervous energy, which he sought to manage (Weisbrode, 2018).

Yet, Ike occasionally used anger (feigned or real) to terminate an unproductive negotiation. Vernon Walters, Ike's NATO interpreter, recounts an instance in which Ike was negotiating an issue with the Italian Defense minister.

The Italian Defense Minister, Pacciardi, insisted that the Greek and Turkish sector of NATO be under an Italian commander. Ike knew that this demand was a non-starter and that he would be unable to negotiate it through to his desired conclusion. Ike feigned indignation and anger at something the defense minister said. Flustered, the Minister then accepted the United States' command of those sectors. Ike later told Walters that he feigned anger as a means of settling the subject by getting the Minister to consent to the United States command as a compromise (Walters, 2001).

Ike was willing to make concessions to strong-willed associates when doing so would get him closer to the goal he was pursuing. Ike's long-standing dealings with the British General Bernard Law Montgomery, 'Monty,' is a good example. Ike often tolerated Monty's insubordination, insults, and arrogance to reach the greater goal of a WWII Allied victory (Eisenhower, 2004). Ike usually refused to attack his political opponents, "I hate this firing back at what the other fellow said. It's the old, old story: you're no bigger a man than the man who can get your goat - no bigger than the things that annoy you" (Hughes, 1963, p. 192).

Although Eisenhower was probably unaware of it, he practiced a variation of negotiation, now known as *Principled Negotiation*. Principled negotiation is codified in the 2011 book, *Getting to Yes*, by Roger Fisher and Bill Ury. Principled negotiation focuses on the *interests of the parties and emphasizes conflict management and conflict resolution*. What Fisher and Ury teach, and what Eisenhower practiced, is that a negotiator always negotiates from a position of strength. Therefore, Eisenhower's variation of Principled Negotiation is called *Strong Negotiation*. Eisenhower almost always negotiated from a position of strength. A position of strength does not mean that you always have the upper hand in a negotiation. Rather, you find your areas of strength and use those areas to your advantage, moving negotiations to those strengths.

According to Fisher and Ury (2011), there are four central guidelines to Principled Negotiation: (1) *Separate people from the problem being negotiated.* Issues should be decided on their merits, rather than being influenced by emotions or by the individuals who are involved. (2) *Focus on the negotiating parties' interests, not their positions.* The underlying interests or motivations that drive individuals in a negotiation are often quite similar. By focusing on interests, the parties may see that they are closer than they thought they were initially. Any discussion about interests should offer concrete and specific details. (3) *Generate different options for mutual gain.* Sometimes people will focus too narrowly when generating ideas. For example, they may judge the ideas during a brainstorming session, rather than simply proposing ideas and evaluating them later. Alternatively, parties may limit their focus to their own immediate interests. This stifles options that have appeal to all involved in the negotiation. (4) *Base the outcome from a principled negotiation session on objective criteria.* For example, if two parties are involved in the purchase and sale of a house, certain objective criteria might be applied to the price, such as the recent sale prices of comparable homes in the area, adjustments for depreciation, or the opinion of an independent appraiser.

While president of the United States, Eisenhower had the advantage of being the head of the strongest nation on earth. One of the most difficult, protracted, complicated, and contentious negotiations that Eisenhower undertook was the Korean Armistice. The Korean Armistice has lasted over 65 years.

Successful, principled negotiation operates from a position of strength. The principled negotiator has integrity, which is power. Integrity is power. Principle is power. And power void of principle creates abuse. Power used with integrity is principled negotiation. Eisenhower had a simple definition of power - *power is the ability to produce the desired result.* "Leadership is the art of getting someone else to do something you want done because he wants to do it," (DDE in Society for Personnel Administration, 1954).

The historian Kenneth Weisbrode writes that at the center of Ike's actions of negotiation is empathy. "An ally or friend empathizes from a position of strength and does so in order to compound and extend that position" (2018, p. 36). Principled and pragmatic use of power is a hallmark of the Eisenhower presidency. Eisenhower practiced *conservation of power.* Conservation of power means that Ike refrained from abusing or throwing his power around.

To further complicate this concept and use of power, there is a contradiction of power that Ike used. In a paradoxical way, Ike said never use force in international affairs. AND, if you must use force, use it overwhelmingly. The following chapters of this book illustrate this principle. First, never use force. Second, if you use force, use it unanswerably, unopen to dispute. The use of force must be irrefutable. Be conclusive, swift, and overwhelming in the use of force. And use that force unemotionally (Eisenhower, 1967, p.2).

The uncontrolled display of emotion in negotiation displays a weakness that will be exploited by your opponent. This includes getting personal. Although getting personal with insults or rebukes may be witty or amusing, it has a negative effect on the outcome of the negotiation. Yet, good humor, good faith, and well-intentioned levity in a tense negotiating situation can be beneficial to the outcome. Eisenhower rarely got personal in his admonitions or arguments. Eisenhower attempted to avoid assuming that he knew what was in another person's heart. According to Eisenhower and his experience in dealing with multiple leaders during WWII and immediately after: "All through my European experience, I learned that you never try to judge people's intentions and if you try to judge them you are almost always wrong. And if you try to condemn them, why then the consequences are often beyond your scope" (Thompson, 1984, p. 134).

Make special note of the words '...why then the consequences are often beyond your scope.' Here Ike demonstrates his clear knowledge that if you scorn and condemn a man, he will almost always retaliate. Furthermore, he will undermine you at any opportunity. As Dale Carnegie, in his book *How to Win Friends and Influence People*, communicates his first principle as "Don't criticize, condemn, or complain." *How to Win Friends and Influence People* has sold over 30 million copies worldwide. The message is simple; don't impugn people's motives (Carnegie, 2009).

When opponents are condemned in a negotiation, they feel wronged. And when we feel wronged individually, we have a greater tendency to lash out, to retaliate at being hurt. Avoiding personal attacks during negotiations displays strength. This may seem counterintuitive because we respond emotionally to displays of angry force. We think these emotional displays of righteous anger and force represent power and strength. Ike once had his assistant Bryce Harlow strike the word 'deliberate' from a statement. Ike said to him, "Never, ever attack a person's motives" (Weisbrode 2018, p. 72). In truth, it takes much greater strength to exercise forbearance when angry or indignant than it does to react. We make the mistake of believing that hitting back twice as hard is a sign of strength. Instead, it is a sign of a lack of self-control and capitulation. The use of positive emotion in negotiation can have a positive effect on the outcome of a situation.

Eisenhower could successfully use emotions in negotiations. Ike was recognized as a fair negotiator, using treatment consistent with "custom, law, organizational practice, and community expectations." Ike was usually honest in his dealings. What he communicated was accurate. Yet Ike recognized that not everyone in a negotiation was entitled to all of the information. This does mean that there is never any intent to deceive or trick. Finally, Ike was "Consistent with Current Circumstances" in his negotiating practice. These "Core Concerns" as they are outlined by Fisher and Shapiro (appreciation, affiliation, autonomy, status, and role), can be used as a way to understand the emotional state of others as well as a way to stimulate positive emotions in the negotiators (Fisher and Shapiro, 2005).

Why is Ike *the Greatest American Statesman*? And what does that designation have to do with being a good negotiator? A statesman is defined as "a person who is experienced in the art of government or versed in the administration of government affairs; a person who exhibits great wisdom and ability in directing the affairs of a government or in dealing with important public issues" (WordReference.com). What we often refer to as leadership qualities are, in fact, skills as a negotiator. The story of Ike's strong negotiation skills as the 34th United States president began as he coolly sought the 1952 Republican Party presidential nomination.

In 1952, the last five presidential elections in the United States had been won by Democrats, four elections by Franklin Delano Roosevelt (FDR) and one by Harry S.

Truman. President Truman's popularity as president suffered due to scandals in his administration, and the Korean War, which became a standoff. His Gallup Poll presidential approval ratings went from a high of 82% (in 1945) to a low of 20% by the beginning of 1952. Truman left the US presidency with an approval rating of about 35%. Truman was a shrewd politician, and he knew that his chances of winning re-election were slim (Pach, 1991).

Truman tried to recruit Ike as the presidential nominee for the Democratic Party. But Ike's personal politics were closer to the Republican Party, and there was a strong movement within the Republican Party to recruit Ike. Ike and Truman generally had a good relationship. However, as conflicting politics began to infuse their relationship, their relationship deteriorated. Truman knew that he would lose if he ran against Ike. Ike was too popular and Truman too unpopular. Ultimately, Truman supported Illinois Governor Adlai Stevenson as the Democratic Party 1952 presidential nominee. Stevenson won the nomination at the Democratic National Convention in Chicago in 1952. The 1952 Democratic Party vice-presidential nominee was Senator John Sparkman of Alabama (Pach, 1991).

The Democratic Party platform of 1952 proposed a strong national defense, collective security against the Soviet Union, multilateral disarmament, repeal of the Taft-Hartley Labor Act, equal employment opportunities for minorities, and public assistance for the aged, children, blind, and the disabled. The platform included the expansion of the nationwide school lunch program and supported efforts to fight racial discrimination (The American Presidency Project). The Democratic Party's effort to fight racial discrimination was belied by the fact that Stevenson's vice-presidential running mate, Alabama Senator John Sparkman, was an outspoken segregationist.

The 1952 Republican Party platform pledged to end the unpopular war in Korea, supported the development of nuclear weapons as a deterrence strategy, and supported retention of the Taft–Hartley Labor Act. It opposed discrimination against race, religion, or national origin. It supported federal action to eliminate lynching and pledged to end communist subversion in the United States (The American Presidency Project).

The Eisenhower campaign summed up the 1952 election as one about Korea, Communism, and Corruption. Eisenhower and Nixon won the election with a strong majority; 55% to 44%, and 442 electoral votes to 89 electoral votes. Stevenson and Sparkman only won 9 states in the South.

Figure 3: Eisenhower 1952 Republican National Convention

The 1956 election was more or less a repeat of the 1952 election, with the exception of Tennessee Senator Estes Kefauver being the running mate of Adlai Stevenson. Eisenhower for president and Nixon for vice-president were once again the Republican Party nominees. The Democratic Party's platform called for voting rights, equal employment opportunities, and the desegregation of public schools. This platform reflected the fact that Kefauver was not a segregationist. The 1956 Republican Party platform included federal assistance to low-income communities, the extension and protection of Social Security, and equal pay for equal work regardless of sex.

The Eisenhower and Nixon ticket won the US Presidency with an even greater majority in 1956; 57% to 42% and 457 electoral votes to 73 electoral votes. Stevenson and Kefauver only won seven states in the South: Missouri, Arkansas, Mississippi, Alabama, Georgia, and the Carolinas (The American Presidency Project). Ike represented the Eastern progressive wing of the Republican party, while Taft represented the Midwestern and Southern conservative wing of the Republican Party. Taft received more votes than Ike in the primaries, with Taft winning about 36% of the primary vote to Ike's ~26%. But Ike was seen as more electable than Taft.

During the two terms of the Eisenhower presidency, there were great threats to the nation. During Ike's fifty-year career, from his first days as a cadet at West Point in 1911 to the end of his second term as the 34th US president in 1961, the world was fraught with upheaval and peril. From the worldwide instability of WWI and WWII to the Cold War and nuclear armaments, Ike negotiated the dangers for US and Allied troops and millions of civilians.

Ike had a resolute reverence for democracy and the will of the people to govern themselves. Yet, Ike did subvert the will of the people at times throughout his career, particularly as president. Ike undermined the will of the people in Iran by supporting the 1953 CIA-directed covert action to overthrow the widely supported Iranian Prime Minister Mohammad Mosaddegh. This US and UK covert action in Iran reinstated the rule of the royal dictator, the Shah of Iran. The Shah of Iran went on to rule Iran until the 1979 Iranian Revolution

In Good Faith

removed him from power. The Shah of Iran remained a principal US ally in the Middle East for twenty-five years.

Ike also subverted the will of the Guatemalan people by directing the CIA to depose the democratically elected Guatemalan President Jacobo Arbenz and install the military dictator Carlos Castillo Armas. Ike was instrumental in providing US financing for the French Colonial War in Vietnam and the establishment of South Vietnam. These covert operations were justified in Ike's view by the need to prevent the spread of Communism. But in these covert operations, Ike's fear of Communism prevented him from respecting the democratic will of millions of people, and he thus supported brutal dictators.

In an odd show of support for the Spanish fascist dictator Generalissimo Franco in 1959, Ike visited him in Madrid to reinforce a US/Spanish pact for US military bases in Spain. Ike wrote about Franco in his memoirs, *Waging Peace*, "My first brief visit with him certainly provided no basis on which to form anything more than a hasty impression, but I found him personable and agreeable-indeed, sufficiently so that I wonder what the consequence would be if he became willing to hold free elections" (1965, p. 510). Franco never held free elections, but he did reign as a Spanish dictator for almost 40 years from 1939 through 1975. Franco brutally repressed the people of Spain and murdered thousands of political dissidents, while he attended Catholic Mass every Sunday, and taught generations of Spanish school children that he was ordained by God to rule them for the rest of his life.

These are massive moral failures by Eisenhower. Ike's covert actions in Iran and Guatemala are indefensible. However, moral and humanitarian violations by Eisenhower do not undermine his actions as a great leader and negotiator. The stories that follow demonstrate that Ike acted in good faith in most of his decisions as the 34th president of the United States.

Ike believed that the Korean conflict was an intractable war. It was a lose-lose situation for almost all parties, where the reasonable course of action for the United States was to bring back the hundreds of thousands of US troops fighting the Korean War. How could Ike do this? How did Ike win the Armistice?

The Suez Crisis was one of the most volatile and contentious crises of the Eisenhower Presidency. Ike got caught somewhat flat-footed by the covert operations of France, the UK, and Israel in their military campaign to repossess the Suez Canal from the Egyptian leader Gamal Abdel Nasser. Nasser had nationalized the Canal on July 26, 1956. Ike respected Nasser, but Ike distrusted him. Ike had to figure out a path that supported democracy in Egypt while respecting the rule of law and maintaining good relations with three US allies - especially France and the UK, with whom the United States had a special relationship.

Ike strongly supported voting rights for African Americans. However, he was sometimes conflicted about the full integration of African Americans into all aspects of white society in the United States. Ike failed to support interracial marriage. Ike believed that the Civil Rights Act of 1957 was long overdue for African Americans and that it was an integral part of the Republican Party platform as well as a campaign promise by Ike.

Ike avoided being a social leader in the US presidency even though he strongly supported civil rights as a matter of a moral imperative as well as expanding the democratic franchise in America. It was not lost on Ike that he received 39% of the African American vote (Presidency of Dwight D.

Eisenhower, 1965). Ike received more African American support than any other US Republican Party presidential candidate. He stood firm on key provisions of the 1957 Civil Rights Act. Ike had to find a way to get the 1957 civil rights bill passed in the US Congress without being the most visible leader of the effort. He worked behind the scenes and enlisted others to get the bill passed.

Ike worked publicly and behind the scenes in negotiations to help resolve the Steel Strike of 1959. Ike was exasperated and even disgusted at times by the narrow-mindedness of both labor and management in the strike. Nonetheless, Ike worked closely with all parties as an honest broker to end the strike and its hard-hitting effects on the US economy (Tiffany, 1988). The tragedy of the strike is that the US steel industry was already in decline at the time of the strike, and the strike accelerated its decline. Ike knew this. Ike was flabbergasted that management believed that domestic steel prices would be maintained by the federal government after the strike. And labor believed that they would ultimately win their wage increase demands.

Ike believed that both sides of the strike were selfish and short-sighted. The inability of labor and management to look beyond their own parochial interests had devastating effects, which were both immediate and long-term. With 500,000 workers off the job and cascading effects across the US economy, there was long-term damage with steel imports overtaking US steel production because of the artificially high cost of steel production in the United States (Tiffany, 1988).

In the U2 incident, Ike and his advisers made fatal mistakes in calculating the need for US intelligence as well as their own inability to engage the Soviets in meaningful negotiations. But to his credit, Ike did sincerely seek to engage the Russians in disarmament. The problem was that in 1960, just before these international disarmament talks were to begin in Paris in May of 1960, a US spy plane was shot down over Soviet airspace by a Soviet surface-to-air missile. The U2 pilot, Francis Gary Powers, survived the crash and was captured by the Soviets. The optics of the incident (the United States repeatedly violating Soviet airspace) were bad, and the whole international fiasco overshadowed any possibility of fruitful negotiations.

Ike's rise as a military leader and his position as the WWII Allied Forces Supreme Commander prepared him to be the 34th US president and a consummate negotiator. *Strong negotiation skills made Ike a great leader.* Ike understood that strong, principled negotiation is a source of great power.

Chapter 2
The 20th Century Korean Armistice: Know When to Call a Fight

"Leadership in the political as well as in other spheres consists largely in making progress through compromise - but it does not mean compromising with basic principles" (DD Eisenhower in a letter to long-time friend Swede Hazlett, 16 October 1952).

The Korean Armistice was signed on July 27, 1953, which resulted in a ceasefire between the belligerents. However, a peace treaty was never signed, so technically North Korea and South Korea are still at war. In April 2018, the leaders of North Korea and South Korea met at the Korean Demilitarized Zone (DMZ) and agreed to work towards a treaty to formally end the Korean War. The Korean War is truly the *War that Never Ended. Armistice* is defined as an agreement made by opposing sides in a war to stop fighting for a certain time, a truce (Dictionary.com).

Eisenhower believed his success in completing the Korean Armistice was his greatest accomplishment as president of the United States. In 1952, at the end of his presidency, Harry S. Truman was very unpopular with a disapproval rating of 66%. Truman may very well have run again in 1952 in the absence of the Korean War (Crabtree, 2003).

Sometimes it is difficult to decide where to start a story. But the story must start somewhere. So in this book we start with the story of the Korean Armistice in the late 1800s. In order to understand the circumstances under which Korea was divided, the war was fought, and the Korean Armistice negotiated, it is relevant to consider the history of the Korean Peninsula.

In Eastern Buddhism, there is a humbling concept called *dependent origination* (*Pali - Paticca-samuppada*). Dependent origination holds that all actions and events arise because of innumerable and complicated preceding circumstances. And there is no way we can understand all the preceding events, but we can seek to understand as much as possible from what we learn. The myriad formations in the causal chain of events that lead to existing circumstances are impossible to fully understand. But in order to better understand existing circumstances, we challenge our existing mental formations or biases (Encyclopedia Britannica). Dependent origination is a good metaphor for our attempts to understand history, and it made negotiations to end the Korean War extraordinarily complex.

Was Eisenhower 'daring not to win but not affording to lose' as a negotiation strategy because of the dependent origination of events he failed to understand? That may be unfair under the circumstances. Yet, in the United States, there was public sentiment against Eisenhower. The US Kiwanis Clubs accused Eisenhower of selling Korea *down the river* and in a derogatory way, referred to the Korean Armistice as the *Eisenhower Peace*. Conservative US Republican and Democratic Party congressmen generally supported General Douglas MacArthur's efforts to expand the Korean War. Support was strong among these congressmen for Generalissimo Chaing Kai-Shek and his opposition to the People's Army of Mao Zedong. Public sentiment was very much in favor of President Truman sending troops in 1950 to Korea to protect South Korea from the North Korean invasion. But within 2 or 3 years, the American public had soured on the Korean War, and public opinion was in favor of bringing home the American troops in Korea (Crabtree, 2003).

Hardline US anti-communists believed that China was lost to the communists because of the failure of will by President Truman, the United Nations, and later Ike and his generals. This view is still held today by many older, hard-edged conservatives (Presidency of Dwight D. Eisenhower).

There are several fundamental strategies and tactics for negotiation:
> (1) Being willing to walk away from the negotiation
> (2) Knowing all your viable options and having a Plan B and Plan C, while keeping all those options on the table as long as possible
> (3) Escalating and expanding the problem
> (4) Understanding what you are willing to trade for the desired outcome, and
> (5) Negotiating on multiple fronts. In the case of the Korean War under the circumstances, Ike considered the Korean Armistice on US terms as a partial victory rather than an overall loss.

Sometimes you negotiate with more people than you expected. Sometimes those who you thought were your allies actively work against you and the objectives of the negotiation. Eisenhower did successfully negotiate the Korean Armistice. However, General Douglas MacArthur claimed that Ike engaged in communist appeasement. Was Ike successful, or were he and his compatriots deluding themselves? To better understand the dependent origination of the Korean War, it is worthwhile to examine Korean history.

For centuries, the Korean Peninsula has been fought over. The Korean people, ancient and modern, have been subjected to many wars over many centuries. The Korean Peninsula is about 85 thousand square miles - North Korea is 46,500 square miles with a population of about 26,000,000 and South Korea is 38,690 square miles with a population of about 51,000,000. North Korea has a per capita income of $1,800 and South Korea has a per capita income of $31,000, seventeen times that of North Korea.

Korea has been invaded from the North and the South. One of the earliest Korean empires was the Kingdom of Joseon, which was a Korean kingdom founded by Yi Seonggye. Korean Dynasties lasted for approximately five centuries, from 1392 to 1897. The dynasty was severely weakened during the late 16th and early 17th centuries. The Japanese invasions of (1592–98) and the first and second Manchu (China) invasions of 1636 nearly overran the Korean Peninsula. This led to an increasingly harsh Korean isolationist policy (still in place for North Korea), for which the country became known as the *Hermit Kingdom*.

Japanese rule of Korea began with the end of the Joseon dynastic monarchy of Korea in 1910 and ended at the conclusion of WWII in 1945. Japanese rule of Korea was the outcome of a process that began with the Japan–Korea Treaty of 1876, which integrated Korea both politically and economically into the Empire of Japan. The Japan–Korea Treaty of 1905 declared the Empire of Korea a protectorate of Japan. The annexation of Korea by Japan was established by the Japan–Korea Treaty of 1910. The Japanese colonized the Korean Peninsula. This brutal Japanese rule further perpetuated the *Japanization of Korea.* Korean enmity toward Japan continues to this day. The Korean Peninsula has undergone five periods of foreign occupation - China,

In Good Faith

the Mongols, Japan, the USSR, and then the United States. The modern division of Korea began in 1943.

In November 1943, at the Cairo Conference with the United States, Great Britain, and China, the attendees held that. "…in due course, Korea shall become free and independent" President Franklin D. Roosevelt wanted a multinational trusteeship for Korea.

Figure 4: 38th Parallel Korean War

After the Japanese empire surrendered and was taken apart at the end of WWII, the Korean Peninsula was caught between the capitalist West and the communist East in the Cold War. It was at the Yalta Conference, in February of 1945, that US President Franklin Delano Roosevelt (FDR) proposed a US/Russian/Chinese control of the Korean Peninsula. In August 1945, the United States divided Korea into the North and the South at the 38th Parallel. Ironically, US officials at that time were unaware that at the turn of the century Russia and Japan had proposed dividing Korea into North and South for control by Russia and Japan. Then in

December 1945, at the Moscow Conference, the United States, USSR, and Great Britain agreed to a trusteeship of Korea and created the Joint Soviet-American Commission. The commission proposed a provisional Korean democratic government.

However, the post-WWII allied ad hoc efforts at Korean independence came to naught. The United States supported the Republic of Korea, which was established in August of 1948. The USSR supported the Democratic People's Republic of Korea, which was established in September of 1948. Both governments claimed control of the entire peninsula. The Americans controlled south of the 38th Parallel Line, and the communists controlled north of the Line. Later the USSR would cede North Korean influence to Mao's Communist China. The USSR's 25th Army took part in the USSR's advancement into North Korea right after WWII. USSR troops remained in North Korea after the end of WWII to help rebuild the country. USSR forces left North Korea in late 1948. The United States viewed North Korea in the context of the Cold War. The United States saw the invasion of South Korea by communist-supported North Korea as an attempt to expand communist control.

In May of 1950, Kim Il-sung visited Mao Zedong and the Chinese leadership in Beijing and discussed his plans to invade South Korea. China entered the Korean War in support of North Korea in October of 1950 and sent the Chinese People's Volunteers to Korea to fight against the United Nations Command (USC). Communist China also received North Korean refugees and students and provided economic aid during the war. China continues to supply North Korea with essential aid.

On June 27, 1950, President Harry S. Truman announced to the people of the United States and the world that the United

States would intervene in the Korean conflict to prevent the invasion of South Korea by North Korean communists. President Truman indicated that Joseph Stalin and the USSR were behind the North Korean invasion. (It was later proven that the USSR had approved the invasion.) The invasion of South Korea by North Korea was fought with USSR tanks and weapons. There was fear that the United States' assistance to South Korea could lead to a broader war between the United States and the USSR. President Truman's decision received overwhelming approval from the US Congress and the US public (A&E Television Networks, LLC). President Truman failed to request a formal declaration of war from Congress, but Congress did vote to extend the military draft and authorized Truman to call up military reservists. President Truman appointed General Douglas MacArthur as commander of all UN forces in Korea.

The United States had a strong desire to keep China out of the conflict, especially Formosa (Taiwan). The forces of the nationalist China leader Chaing Kai-shek, located in Formosa, were prepared to enter the Korean conflict opposing the Chinese Communist forces of Mao Zedong (National Archives). At this time, the stated UN objective in Korea was "...to bring about the complete independence and unity of Korea in accordance with the General Assembly resolutions of November 14, 1947, December 12, 1948, and October 21, 1949" (National Archives). However, President Truman had to walk a line between United States support for Korean unification and the threat of a larger war.

Indeed, Truman and the US NSC were adamant about no US troops being used in any fighting in the North-Eastern province of North Korea bordering the USSR or in the area along the Manchurian border. General Douglas MacArthur viewed it very differently. MacArthur fervently believed that the Communist expansion into all of Asia including Korea must be fought with all the US military might. To General MacArthur, this included a naval blockade against the China coast, unrestricted flights in Chinese coastal areas, and bringing the forces of Chiang Kai-shek into the war to fight against the forces of the common communist enemy. MacArthur had strong Congressional support from hardline Republicans and Southern Democrats to widen the Korean War. There was also a fair amount of anti-communist US public support. MacArthur used this vocal support effectively, to pursue his aims of broadening the conflict to become a land war in Asia.

MacArthur prosecuted his cause by claiming that there were communist sympathizers in the Truman administration and within the ranks of the US government. General Douglas MacArthur claimed that these forces within the US government were preventing him from vanquishing the enemy by expanding the Korean War into China. Increasingly, General MacArthur's public pronouncements on the Korean War were defying the explicit orders of the US Commander in Chief and the US Joint Chiefs of Staff (A&E Television Networks, LLC).

General of the Army and Chairman of the Joint Chiefs of Staff, Omar Bradley, communicated that the real benefactors in an expanded US war with China would be the USSR. The USSR would benefit by not being in the war, but at the same time being the overall recipients of a weakened US military force. General Bradley stated, "Frankly, in the opinion of the Joint Chiefs of Staff, this strategy would involve us in the wrong war, in the wrong place, at the wrong time, and with the wrong enemy" (US Senate Committees on Armed Services and Foreign Relations, 1951, p. 732).

In Good Faith

The United States was caught unprepared in the North Korean invasion of South Korea. Truman and the United Nations had to scramble to respond with police action. In his book *Diplomacy*, Secretary of State Henry Kissinger contends that China, North Korea, and the USSR were surprised with the large defense response by the US/UN to the invasion of South Korea by North Korea (2012). According to the memoirs of Nikita Khrushchev, USSR Premiere, the invasion of North Korea was the creation of Kim Il Sung (who was the USSR designated leader of the Democratic Front for the Reunification of the Fatherland). Joseph Stalin went along with the invasion because Stalin supposedly thought it would be an easy invasion (2012).

The United States lacked a clear military objective early on in Korea, other than pushing the North Korean forces out of South Korea and in general, repelling aggression. General Douglas MacArthur sought to stop the early stalemate and landed US forces at Inchon (the port of Seoul) and thus cut North Korea supply lines with Pyongyang. After this, the North Korean Army collapsed, and the United States had a major victory in the fight against communist aggression (National Archives).

After the Chinese entered the war, in November 1950, the United States backtracked on Korean unification and again stated that the United States' goal was to put down aggression. Kissinger also states in his memoirs that Chairman Mao wanted to expel US forces altogether from the Korean Peninsula (2012). Modifying his stand on Korea, President Truman then said in April of 1951 that the United States was trying to keep the Korean conflict from spreading to other areas. In his memoirs, Kissinger writes that America's leaders thought that they understood the dangers of escalating the Korean War, but that these same leaders failed to understand the penalties of stalemate (2012).

General Douglas MacArthur pushed the issue and asked, was there any choice between stalemate and all-out war? The debate broke out in the public and President Truman had no choice but to dismiss a publicly insubordinate commander. It was at this point President Truman shifted his public rhetoric on Korea away from the concept of repelling aggression. First, he maintained that the fighting must stop. Second, concrete steps must be taken to ensure that the fighting would be prevented from starting again. Third, there must be an end to the aggression. President Truman went on to state a settlement founded upon these elements would open the way for the unification of Korea and the withdrawal of all foreign forces. Under these circumstances, we can concede that MacArthur did have a point when he argued against stalemate as a foreign policy in Korea. Although attrition was an unofficial policy - an unformed approach whereby the United States sought to gradually reduce the strength and effectiveness of the North Korean and Chinese forces through sustained attack and pressure.

Henry Kissinger writes that President Truman rejected General Douglas MacArthur's alternative and believed the only viable strategy was a stalemate. General Omar Bradley, Chairman of the US Joints Chief of Staff, stated that without a commitment of great forces the course was narrowly getting North Korea out of South Korea (2012). Henry Kissinger accurately stated about the United States in Korea, "if the US dared not to win but could not afford to lose, what were its options? - daring not to win but not affording to lose" (2012, p. 486).

Ultimately President Truman conceded the following constrained view on the Korean War - "Every decision I made in connection with the Korean conflict has this one aim in mind: to prevent world war and the terrible destruction it would bring to the civilized world. This meant that we should not do anything that would provide an excuse to the USSR and plunge the free nations into full-scale all-out-war" (Truman, 1956, p. 345). Henry Kissinger further points out that at no point during the Korean conflict did the USSR threaten to enter the war, and in June 1951 the Chinese and Korean communists proposed negotiations and the United States halted offensive actions. It is through this action (US halting of offensive actions), according to Kissinger, the United States lost leverage in the negotiations for a Korean Armistice (Kissinger, 2012).

"In fact, in most negotiations, unilateral gestures remove a key negotiating asset," Kissinger states. "Typically, it is the pressure on the battlefield that generates the negotiation," Reducing the pressure reduces the enemy's incentive to negotiate. Kissinger writes that this is what happened in Korea. US restraint in pushing back the Chinese allowed North Korea to remain. "This led to a drawn-out war of attrition, which was brought to a halt only because a painful equilibrium emerged between China's physical limitations and America's psychological inhibitions" (Kissinger, 2012, p. 489).

To Truman, there was a very narrow path between resisting aggression and avoiding a larger war. It was very difficult here to claim that the United States achieved its goal. But General Dwight David Eisenhower, as the 1952 Republican presidential nominee on the campaign trail, wanted to change this view. Eisenhower believed very strongly that President Truman had failed in his solemn responsibility as the US Commander in Chief to bring the Korean War to an end. Ike exploited the US public sentiment against the Korean War. Ike made his criticism of the Korean War a central theme of his 1952 presidential campaign.

The 1952 Republican Party platform pledged to end the unpopular war in Korea and supported the development of nuclear weapons as a deterrence strategy. Another plank in the platform, inspired by the anti-communism crusade of the time, was to fire all the loafers, incompetents, and unnecessary employees at the State Department. Ike took his strong 1952 US presidential victory as a mandate to get out of Korea as soon as possible. Senator Karl Mundt of South Dakota, co-chair of the Republican Party Speakers Bureau, had a clever formula during the 1952 presidential campaign 'K1C2' - K was of the Korean War and C2 was for Communism and Corruption. The Republican Party blamed the Democratic Party for the Korean War (or stalemate as it was seen). This K1C2 theme failed to take off. However, the phrase, "Eisenhower - turning the world toward peace" did resonate with voters, as Eisenhower was viewed as the US representative force behind the allied victory in Europe in 1945, and the peace and stability that followed (The American Presidency Project).

The American people also believed the war in Korea had become a stalemate. Public sentiment, which supported the initial US troop deployment to Korea, turned against further involvement. Eisenhower used public sentiment against the war to his advantage. As noted, a major theme of his campaign was that the Democrats had mishandled the war. Ike claimed that President Truman and the Democrats in power were insufficiently prepared for war. And therefore, according to Ike, the Korean War was in a bloody stalemate. On the campaign trail, Ike promised the American people that if elected, he would find a way to end the Korean War. Ike's campaign promise was to end the war in Korea. Critics claimed this was an empty promise.

While campaigning in 1952, Eisenhower became convinced that Americans wanted to end the Korean War. Contrast this with the fact that when President Harry S. Truman first sent US ground troops into Korea on June 30, 1950, seventy-eight percent of Americans said they approved of Truman's decision to send military aid, and only 15% disapproved. However, public support eroded, and by early 1951 about half of Americans thought that sending troops to Korea was a mistake. It is interesting to note that during the Korean War, about half of Americans thought that the Korean War would lead to WWIII. Having had two world wars in the last fifty years led Americans to pessimism about the prospects for the survival of humanity (The American Presidency Project).

However, public opinion can be fickle and by January 1953, soon after Eisenhower was elected and truce talks began again, American public opinion shifted yet again, with half of Americans saying the war was right, while a low of 36% said it was a mistake. By May 1953, the public seemed to shift again as 74% of Americans believed a satisfactory agreement was unattainable. Further demonstrating Americans' exhaustion with the war, 69% of Americans in April 1953 approved of a Korean Armistice signing based on the Korean War being halted at the 39th Parallel. This, along with overwhelming support of how Eisenhower was handling the Korean War, with 80% of Americans approving of Ike's handling.

These numbers add up to the mandate that Ike saw from the American people to end the Korean War. Indeed, through conversations with numerous military personnel and political leaders, Eisenhower communicated his belief that Americans had elected him to bring the US troops home from Korea. Eisenhower told the American people in 1952, while he was campaigning, the first thing he would do after being elected president, would be to go to the front lines in Korea to see for himself what it was like. And he did. Ike's campaign devised the "I will go to Korea" speech, which gave Ike options. When Ike saw the speech, he said that he had already made up his mind to go to Korea and see for himself what was happening there. Ike was opposed to an immediate ending to the war.

However, the conservative wing of the Republican Party, the hawks, said that Ike was selling Korea down the river by winding down the war and being weak with North Korea, China, and the USSR. Ike's critics on the right derisively referred to the Armistice as the Eisenhower Peace. Others called it a *Far Eastern Munich*. There is some truth to this as, aside from outright aggression, the communists refused to abide by the Armistice agreement. The question worth asking is whether, with greater use of military force by the United States, "Could the communists have been forced into accepting reunification?" Maybe General Douglas MacArthur was right in his push to expand the Korean War.

Then there were groups such as the Save Our Sons Committee, which supported Ike in the ceasefire. The South Korean Progressive Party supported the truce and opposed attempts by Rhee to have more from North Korea. However, many hardline Republicans also opposed the truce and supported Syngman Rhee. Many Veterans Associations also opposed the Truce. The powerful South Carolina Democratic Party politician Strom Thurman (who supported President Eisenhower for president in 1952) sent a letter to Eisenhower requesting that Ike provide South Korea with weapons and support to expand the war and defeat the communists.

The US Kiwanis and Rotary Clubs opposed giving the communists a compromise in Korea when we could have a victory. While the Save Our Sons Committee called for a ceasefire, a vocal US minority called the Korean Armistice appeasement or craven surrender. One woman sent Ike a telegram that stated that her son was missing in Korea and that the United States must win an honorable peace. Another woman whose son died in Korea told Ike that the Armistice "deprives me of my pride in his sacrifice" (Eisenhower, 1952). The letters to the White House were 3 or 4 to 1 against the Korean Armistice. However, in April of 1953, two-thirds of Americans supported signing the Korean Armistice when it came time to do so.

Figure 5: Eisenhower visit to Korea - Christmas 1952

Eisenhower criticized the Truman administration over Korea. Ike seldom attacked his political foes with such force. However, in a Detroit 1952 campaign speech, one of the least known and most important in US history, Ike presents a damning case against the Truman administration. Ike condemns President Truman for withdrawing US troops from the Korean Peninsula and failing to support the Chinese anti-communist forces of Chaing Kai-shek. Ike was merciless in his condemnation of the abysmal Truman administration leadership in Korea, "There is a Korean War- and we are fighting it - for the simplest of reasons: Because free leadership failed to check and to turn back communist ambition before it savagely attacked us. The Korean War – more perhaps than any other war in history-simply and swiftly followed the collapse of our political defenses. There is no other reason than this: We failed to read and to outwit the totalitarian mind" (Eisenhower, 1952, p. 1).

The October 24, 1952 speech in Detroit contained the following passage:
> "The first task of a new Administration will be to review and re-examine every course of action open to us with one goal in view: To bring the Korean War to an early and honorable end. That is my pledge to the American people… Carefully, then, this new Administration, unfettered by past decisions and inherited mistakes, can review every factor - military, political, and psychological - to be mobilized in speeding a just peace... Progress along at least two lines can instantly begin. First, we can step up the program of training and arming the South Korean forces. Manifestly, under the circumstances of today, United Nations forces cannot abandon that unhappy land. But just as troops of the Republic of Korea covet and deserve the honor of defending their frontiers, so should we give them maximum assistance to ensure their ability to do so" (Eisenhower, 1952, pp. 4-6).

Ike made good on every pledge he made in that fateful speech. Indeed, as we will see later, Ike's exhaustive examination of ALL the possible options in Korea was an extraordinary undertaking. As a negotiator, Ike was as prepared as he could possibly be. As much as he could, Ike examined every imaginable scenario in Korea. He wanted everything on the table. A lesser negotiator would have considered several possibilities and then made a hasty decision because of the pressure of more deaths every day and a general public exhausted with the war.

Immediately after the 1952 presidential election, Eisenhower contacted his long-standing colleague, General Mark Clark. Ike and Clark were in school together at West Point. Ike had made the campaign promise in 1952 to go to Korea, and implicit in this promise was that Ike would seek to bring the Korean conflict to a close. Ike asked Clark to coordinate the trip. On November 29, just a couple of weeks after his election, Eisenhower went to Korea with General Omar Bradley, Chairman of the Joints Chief of Staff, and Charles Wilson, who became the new US secretary of defense. Ike met his son, John, who was an army major serving at the Korean front. Eisenhower was dispirited by his visit. The enemy was entrenched, and a direct assault would result in a very heavy loss of life. It was a sobering visit for Ike - the political attacks on the campaign trail gave way to the harsh reality of the Korean War on the ground (Eisenhower, p. 178).

Ike also visited with South Korean leader Syngman Rhee. Ike realized that Rhee would keep alive his dream of a unified Korea, and Ike also realized the Korean War was unwinnable in its current state. The parties involved would be brought to the table through ongoing pressure on the battlefield, or the war would be expanded significantly, perhaps even using atomic weapons. Ike considered the Korean War an endless battle for barren real estate. Ultimately, South Korea under Rhee never signed the Armistice, and the South Korean leader Syngman Rhee refused to accept the division of Korea (Stokesbury, 1988).

On his way back from Korea, Ike issued a press release that seemed to implicitly threaten a widening of the Korean War. Here we witness an important negotiating tactic. Avoid issuing explicit threats and failing to keep all your options open. Eisenhower refused to close off any options. As Ike once referred to his decision-making process, "I guess I'm just too stubborn to act until all of the necessary facts are in" (Eisenhower and Corbin, 1969, p.195).

Ike and MacArthur met in New York on December 17, 1952, and MacArthur gave Ike a 14-point plan on ending the Korean War - MacArthur advised that the war be escalated to Moscow (Stassen and Houts, 1990, p. 101). MacArthur suggested that Ike meet with Stalin and demand that North Korea and South Korea and East Germany and West Germany be reunified. MacArthur went on to tell Ike that he should communicate to Stalin that if these and other demands are not met, the United States would clear all of Korea of enemy forces with conventional or atomic warfare methods, along with a US commitment to the destruction of China's airfields and industrial centers. Ike clearly understood the implications of implementing MacArthur's 14-Point Plan - likely WWIII. MacArthur was never again consulted by Ike on the Korean War. Ike considered MacArthur's plan lunacy. MacArthur felt bitter about being rebuffed by Ike and later commented, "...he (Ike) doesn't have the guts to make a policy decision. He never did have the guts and he never will" (Ike and MacArthur meeting Waldorf Astoria, NYC, Dec. 1952).

Ike had to Negotiate the Korean Armistice with Multiple Parties. The parties with whom Eisenhower had to negotiate the Korean Armistice were: (1) <u>Syngman Rhee</u> - strongman leader of South Korea - a forceful patriot who opposed the Armistice (South Korea never signed the Armistice) because it failed to unite Korea. Rhee pressured the United States and the United Nations to lead a war that would reunify Korea; (2) The US Congress - most US congresspersons wanted the Korean War to end and supported the Armistice. Some hawks in Congress were unsupportive of the Armistice and wanted to widen the war to include Mainland China; (3) The American People - public opinion was very much in favor of the Armistice by 1953. However, there was a very vocal and strong minority that wanted to expand the war to Mainland China and unify Korea; (4) The Eisenhower administration - John Foster Dulles generally supported the Armistice. However, Dulles did so somewhat reluctantly as he was fiercely anti-communist and saw the opportunity in the Korean War to defeat the Chinese Communist Regime; (5) North Korea - (China) it appears that once North Korea/China hit a stalemate on subsuming South Korea, that there was less and less appetite for escalating or widening the war with South Korea and the United States; (6) The United Nations - the United Nations very much favored the Armistice and an end to the bloodshed.

The Eisenhower administration sought to prevent Syngman Rhee from resuming the war with North Korea by telling him that economic aid would end if Rhee did so. Ike very vigorously sought to prevent Rhee and the ROK from resuming military actions against North Korea. The US Joint Chiefs of Staff believed that was the ROK to successfully engage North Korea in the resumption of an all-out war, that the United States could quickly be drawn into a major world war with China and possibly the USSR.

Fifteen foreign nations other than the United States and South Korea sent combat forces to serve in the United Nations Command in Korea during the Korean War. Five non-combatant nations provided hospitals or ambulance units. Approximately 150,000 foreign servicemen fought, and foreign casualties included 3,360 killed, 11,886 wounded, and 1,801 servicemen missing in action. These forces included Australia, Canada, New Zealand, and the United Kingdom comprised the British Commonwealth Forces. Belgium, Luxembourg, Colombia, Ethiopia, France, Greece, the Netherlands, the Philippines, and Thailand had battalion-sized units attached to the US army divisions; Turkey deployed an infantry brigade.

The Korean War Armistice talks continued through the summer of 1951 with very little progress. The United States bombed Pyongyang in July of 1951 in North Korea to force the negotiations. The bombing failed to improve the negotiations. In August of 1951, the North Korean communists claimed that the UN forces had illegally entered the neutral Kaesong zone. The North Korean communists stopped negotiating, and the talks at Kaesong ended with zero progress.

In October of 1951, the North Korean communists were ready to start negotiating again. Both sides agreed to move negotiations to a new location at Panmunjom. The negotiations resumed in Panmunjom in October of 1951. A few concessions were made, the North Korean communists gave up their demand for a North/South division line on the 38th Parallel and agreed to a border slightly to the North. The United States in turn agreed that North Korea would claim the City of Kaesong on the North Korean/South Korean border. The negotiations then came to an impasse over the issue of what to do with Prisoners of War (POWs). The North Korean and Chinese Communist troops suffered a severe disease epidemic and accused the US forces of biological warfare. The American negotiator in Panmunjom, Admiral C. Turner Joy, was so fed-up with the negotiations that he requested he be replaced.

In Good Faith

In April of 1952, the United States offered new terms to the North Korean communists. If the North Korean communists would permit the United States, United Nations, and the Republic of Korea to give their North Korean Communist POWs a choice to repatriate to North Korea or China or stay in South Korea, then the United States would allow the North Koreans to rebuild and maintain their airbases. This was a hard bargain and a real threat to the North Koreans. The negotiations slowed, and in June of 1952, the United States began bombing the hydroelectric power plants on the Yalu River. The United States sent bombers again to Pyongyang. By October of 1952, just before Eisenhower was elected, as the 34th president of the United States, the Korean War Armistice was out of touch (Stokesbury, 1988).

By May 25, 1953, the UN negotiators presented the 'final offer' to the North Korean communists. The following six weeks were some of the heaviest fighting of the Korean War, with the highest death counts of the war in June of 1953. There were 74 MiGs (USSR jet fighters) downed by the United States Air Force (Stokesbury, 1988). It seemed the closer the Korean Armistice appeared to the adversaries, the more frustrated Syngman Rhee became and the more he tried to sabotage the Armistice. Rhee's dream of Korean unification became more and more impossible.

The North Korean communists decided to dig in. During the night of July 13, 1953, six Chinese divisions assaulted the battle line held by the Republic of Korea II Corps in Central Korea. The North Koreans pushed the South Koreans back about six miles. The North Korean communists claimed a victory and demonstrated they would be willing to continue the fight. Ike had to examine all the options for Korea.

A Memorandum for the US National Security Council (NSC) dated July 17, 1953, states that if the Korean

Armistice is successful, the United States should continue to request support from other forces that are part of the United Nations Command. If the Korean Armistice fails, the Best Alternative to A Negotiated Agreement (BATNA) is for the United States to solicit greater military support from the United Nations coalition forces for Korea.

The US National Security Council developed pros and cons on possible courses of action in Korea on April 2, 1953. The report noted that the Chinese communist authorities had declared via radio on March 30, 1953, that Korean Armistice negotiations should resume. Along with the objective, timing and built up, casualties, cost in billions, enemy reaction, Allies' views, and military appraisal, the US NSC possible courses of action included: (A) Business as Usual (BAU) - continue the current level of operations with limited redeployment of US Forces. (B) Step Up Ground operations to force the Korean Armistice. (C) Step Up Ground operations with a major military offensive forcing the Korean Armistice. (D) Air Attack and a naval blockade against China with possible ground military operations increase forcing the Korean Armistice. (E) Offensive to Korean Peninsula 'waist' (Military Demarcation Line) plus a naval blockade combined with air and naval attacks against China forcing the Korean Armistice. (F) A large-scale military offensive plus a naval blockade and air and naval attacks leading to the goal of a Unified Korea. (1= A, B, C; 2 = D, E, F).

According to these six options, the NSC had casualty estimates from 0 - 400,000 for the United States, Republic of Korea, and Allied forces. The NSC report states that "excluding resort to global war, or complete withdrawal of US forces from Korea, or yielding to the communist position of prisoners of war in the Armistice negotiations, there are two major alternative courses of action open to the United

States in Korea. The first alternative maintains current restrictions on military operations; the second removes these restrictions" (The US National Security Council, Status of Projects January 1, 1954, Possible Courses of Action in Korea).

Figure 6: Colonel-level discussions between the United States and North Korean militaries on October 11, 1951, U.S. National Archives and Records Administration.

From Jan 1953 to July 1953, Korea was the most prominent subject in the NSC meetings. Ike required his military leaders to prepare scenarios whereby the Korean War would be escalated and won (the problem expanded) or ended with some kind of diplomacy. The Russian Dictator Joseph Stalin seemed glad that the war was dragging on and draining the United States, even though Moscow was contributing very little if anything to the war. However, people in China and North Korea were unhappy with prolonging the war. Ike knew from public relations, national politics, and social position that Americans were losing patience with the war. The public wanted Ike to end the War and end it without more US casualties. Ike knew that Korean unification really was a very long shot. One question yet unanswered is whether Korean unification was an implicit or explicit part of the Armistice negotiations (Thomas, 2012).

It was only three weeks into the Ike presidency that the use of nuclear weapons in Korea came up. China was building up troops around Kaesong, and maybe Ike was using the threat of nukes to leverage more Allied support for the UN forces. According to Oral History of John Eisenhower, Eisenhower's son, Ike did consider using tactical nuclear weapons in Korea. According to this oral history, John Eisenhower considered this a real threat from Ike. Eisenhower was a believer in overwhelming force - if you must fight, then fight all the way. This was an overriding principle in the US offense in WWII - use massive US firepower in an overwhelming assault (Edwin, 1967). However, even with the ultimate goal of Korean unification, a massive expansion of the Korean War was just too risky for a world war with China and the USSR. On the 19th of March in 1953 (after the death of Stalin) the USSR Council of Ministers sent a letter to Chairman Mao of China and Kim Il Sung of North Korea indicating their support for the Korean Armistice (Thomas, 2012, p. 74).

Korean Armistice negotiations slowed again in May of 1953, and the battles continued as the stalemate worsened. In May of 1953, Ike and the NSC continued to meet and indicated that they were considering the use of atomic weapons to end the Korean War. Through various unofficial diplomatic channels (Dulles to Indian Prime Minister), it was communicated to the Chinese and the USSR that the United States was considering using atomic weapons. Later, there were some in the Ike administration, that indicated they thought this was why the Chinese and the North Koreans were more willing to negotiate (Eisenhower, Galambos, and Van Ee, 2001).

However, maybe it was more likely that conventional attacks, and the threat of larger conventional attacks, may have made the Chinese and North Koreans more likely to come to the table. In May of 1953, US warplanes started bombing hydro plants, dams, and irrigation canals. Much of North Korea was without power and flooded. Crops were destroyed which led to famine. These comments coincided with instructions that Ike gave to General Mark Clark to make the enemy suffer to get them to the table to sign the Armistice.

Ike knew that the threat of atomic weapons was strong coercion. A few days after the NSC approved a war plan that could include nuclear weapons, the North Korean communists accepted the US/UN peace terms. Ike's Chief of Staff, Sherman Adams, claims that when Ike was asked how the Korean Armistice was achieved, Ike responded with "Danger of an atomic war." Although this comment by Ike is uncorroborated, Adams repeated it (1961). In his Oral History, John Eisenhower claims that it was more so the death of Stalin that pushed the North Korean communists and China to accept the Korean Armistice. After all, it was Joseph Stalin who was considered to have given tacit approval to Kim to invade the South (Edwin, 1967).

Harold Stassen served in the Eisenhower administration in various capacities, including director of the Mutual Security Administration (foreign aid) and special assistant to the president for Disarmament. According to Stassen, he and other cabinet members also considered several options for Korea (Stassen and Houts, 1990, pp. 74 - 75). (1) The military Hawks said to use atomic bombs on North Korea and Red China. (2) United States withdrawal from South

Korea immediately. (3) Restore the leadership of General Douglas MacArthur and give him total control. (4) Turn South Korea back to 100% United Nations control. (5) Withdraw all US forces and let South Korean troops take over. (6) Negotiate a truce immediately. In Appendix A of the NSC, it is stated, "Agreement has been reached in all of the major points of the armistice agreement" (US National Security Council, 1953).

When Ike took office, he also ordered the Joint Chiefs of Staff (JCS) to study the military consequences of Korea - the casualties, cost, manpower needs, equipment needs, and time frames. The results of the JCS study were as follows: (1) Maintain the current stalemate with sporadic and intense fighting. (2) Withdraw US and UN forces and leave Korea to the Republic of Korea Army (ROK). (3) Attempt to drive the North Korean military to the Yalu River repeating General MacArthur's short-lived victory of two years earlier. (4) Try to bring Nationalist China (Chiang Kai-shek) into the war. (5) Broaden the war and bomb parts of China and Manchuria (Stassen and Houts, 1990, p. 207).

Harold Stassen wrote that he visited Ike and after Ike read the JCS report, Ike said that a total victory appeared out, and a frontal assault would produce too many casualties because the communists were too dug in (Stassen and Houts, 1990). As Ike and the JCS concluded, the only option for total victory was saturation bombing of enemy staging areas, including depots across the Yalu River and airfields in Manchuria. It was determined too risky if the ultimate objective was only Korean reunification.

The strategy of hurting the enemy on the field was in keeping the communists at the negotiating table. And so the Korean Armistice proceeded, albeit with fits and starts. However, Ike understood the necessity of using military force to get the North Koreans to the Armistice. According to an oral history interview with General Mark Clark, Ike stated, "There's only one way to get an armistice, and that's by hurting him (North Korean enemy) and the more you hurt him, the quicker you're going to get the armistice" (Luter, 1970, p. 40).

Ike concluded that the catastrophic dangers inherent in expanding and intensifying the conflict were too great a threat. There had been too much retrenchment on the part of the North Koreans for any hope of reunification. It is important to note here that the threat of nuclear war had been omnipresent with the North Koreans since the 38th parallel was established. North Korea continued to use the threat of nuclear retaliation to coerce the world powers, especially the United States, into certain social and economic concessions. The Korean War has never ended - but the Korean Armistice holds almost 70 years later. Ike finally concluded that the single most effective means out of the war would be a negotiated truce. Ike understood that this left Korea split almost along the present lines. Unfortunately, this was almost the same as before the war (Eisenhower, Galambos, and Van Ee, 2001).

Ike distrusted his North Korean adversaries. Although Ike would probably say that he could trust the North Koreans to act in their own self-interest, which may be in line with or contrary to American self-interests or Chinese or South Korean interests. At the same time, Ike had a healthy skepticism of the South Korean leaders' words and actions. Eisenhower also had an abiding wariness of military solutions provided by military leaders. Once when DDE was asked by a reporter about Chinese peace overtures regarding North Korea, Ike replied, "We should take at face value every offer made to us, until it is proved not to be worthy of being so taken" (Eisenhower, 1963p. 147). This is an essential statement in negotiations as it assumes that your opponent is negotiating in good faith unless or until that opponent demonstrates otherwise. Ike may have been a little coy here since Ike was generally wary of the North Korean and Red Chinese overtures.

Maybe Ike took the United States away from the Korean conflict with dishonor. Ike failed to negotiate with the North Koreans using a much more hardline approach. There were a few who believed so. Congressional Republicans and Senator Taft, and even members of Ike's staff, including Dulles and Wilson, believed that the Korean Conflict should have been escalated and the North Koreans should have been completely defeated. In February of 1953, Ike directed UN Commander General Mark Clark (who succeeded General Matthew Ridgway) to begin armistice negotiations; and six months later, the Korean Armistice was signed with little fanfare.

Some of the technical points of the Armistice included: (1) the exact locations of the battle lines, (2) the protection of each side from the other against potential future troop build-ups, (3) policing of the cease-fire, (4) and, the most difficult point, the repatriation of prisoners. **Syngman** Rhee insisted that there would be no forced return to North Korea of any prisoners, same with North Korea to South Korea. Rhee's insistence on this point almost collapsed the talks.

Indeed, according to the notes of the NSC meeting of June 19, 1953, Ike stated that **Syngman** Rhee sought to sabotage the Armistice negotiations and that Rhee wanted to keep fighting. On June 18, Rhee released about 25,000 prisoners of war. He just let them go without following the protocol agreed to as part of the Armistice. The communists broke off talks but did return within a couple of weeks. Dulles contended that the communists wanted the Armistice so much that they would overlook the Rhee release of 25,000 North Korean prisoners (US National Security Council and Eisenhower).

Rhee was publicly rebuked by the Eisenhower administration and given an ultimatum - shape up or the United States will pull its support of South Korea. The unification of Korea was a second-order concern for Eisenhower. Ending the Korean War and bringing US troops back was first, along with keeping China's communism at bay. Ike told his advisors the United States must trust Rhee going forward and even if the United States had to pull out, other US forces would be able to create a defensible perimeter for South Korea. Ike sent a letter to Rhee, chastising his actions, but allowing him to save face. Ike sent Assistant Secretary of State Walter S. Robertson to Korea to tell Rhee personally to get in line or the United States would withdraw troops and withhold aid. Vice President Richard Nixon claimed that the United States must stay militarily in Korea, or it would be a big victory for the 'commies' (Eisenhower, 1965).

Indeed, the greatest obstacle to signing the Armistice had become Syngman Rhee rather than the North Koreans. In negotiations with an adversary, you may have to deal with negotiations from your right and left flank as well. When the United Nations indicated that it would agree to the Armistice on the 39th parallel, Rhee threatened to withdraw the South Korean Army from the UN command. Eisenhower then cut off supplies of fuel and munitions to the South Korean Army, and three weeks later, Rhee capitulated and issued a statement that he would cooperate.

However, as the signing of the Korean Armistice approached, the frustration of Rhee increased. Rhee despised the Korean Armistice and sought to sabotage the talks. Rhee wanted all the support from the United States as well as the reunification. Rhee became a more bitter man as the likelihood of reunification receded (Stokesbury, 1988). Eisenhower soberly stated that "Three Years of Heroism, frustration and bloodshed were over" (Eisenhower, 1963, p. 191).

By May 25, a 'final offer' was proposed to the communists: (1) There would be a five-nation repatriation commission (consisting of India, Poland, Switzerland, Czechoslovakia, and Sweden) with India to supply troops, (2) there would be 90 days for explanations of the repatriations, and (3) there would be limits on the number of explainers.

By April 1953, 70% of Americans supported the Armistice, and 80% of Americans approved of how Ike was handling Korea. This support is unprecedented. As noted, Ike believed that he had a mandate from the American people to bring American soldiers home. Yet, as we witness from Ike's pronouncements, interactions, and analysis, Ike saw no reasonable and justifiable path to winning the Korean War, let alone reunifying North Korea and South Korea. Perhaps he didn't take his own advice and expand the problem of the Korean War in order to solve it (Crabtree, 2003).

The communists said that they would think about the proposal. Finally, the communists agreed to avoid involuntary repatriation. The United States was immovable on the repatriation issue. The North Korean communists and the Communist Chinese were also entrenched on this issue but were eventually forced by military means to concede the issue. This is an essential element of the Korean Armistice. After WWII, many Russian POWs were repatriated to the USSR, and Joseph Stalin had many of them killed. The United States wanted to prevent a repeat of this with the North Korean POWs.

In Good Faith

The United Nations Command and the Chinese-North Korean Command signed the Korean Armistice Agreement on July 27, 1953. The Korean War Armistice established the Military Armistice Commission (MAC), consisting of representatives of the two signatories, to supervise the implementation of the Korean Armistice terms, and the Neutral Nations Supervisory Commission (NNSC) to monitor the Armistice's restrictions on the parties reinforcing or rearming themselves. The North Korean Chinese MAC has since been replaced by Panmunjom representatives under exclusive North Korean management.

Preamble (Korean Armistice):
> The undersigned, the Commander-in-Chief, United Nations Command, on the one hand, and the Supreme Commander of the Korean People's Army and the Commander of the Chinese People's Volunteers, on the other hand, in the interest of stopping the Korean conflict, with its great toil of suffering and bloodshed on both sides, and with the objective of establishing an armistice which will ensure a complete cessation of hostilities and all acts of armed force in Korea until a final peaceful settlement is achieved, do individually, collectively, and mutually agree to accept and to be bound and governed by the conditions and terms of armistice outlined in the following articles and paragraphs, which said conditions and terms are intended to be purely military in character and to pertain solely to the belligerents in Korea (www.ourdocuments.gov).

Finally, it was agreed upon to sign the Korean Armistice at 10 AM on July 27, 1953. The signing took 12 minutes, no handshakes, no words (Stokesbury, 1988). Three of the four major parties signed the Armistice agreement. The Republic of Korea under Rhee refused to sign the Korean Armistice. The 1953 ceasefire agreement still holds the peace between North Korea and South Korea, along with the 2.5-mile undulating demilitarized zone.

"Whenever I run into a problem I can't solve, I always make it bigger. I can never solve it by trying to make it smaller, but if I make it big enough, I can begin to see the outlines of a solution," DDE (Attributed). Ike examined all of the options for ending the Korean War. In his memoir, Ike asserts that he broke the negotiation deadlock in the Korean Armistice by discreetly threatening the North Koreans and the Chinese that the United States would use the atomic bomb in Korea. The Chinese and the North Koreans failed to acknowledge this implied threat. It may be safe to say that the supposed United States threat to use the atomic bomb did play a part in the North Korean communists and the Chinese in signing the Armistice. (Perhaps MacArthur was not all wrong). There were no victories to be gained by North Korea and China refusing to sign the Korean Armistice. And there was little for the United States to gain in refusing to sign the Armistice. So, the North Korean communists and the Chinese finally agreed to the repatriation terms. It does not seem that there was much to gain from this concession.

The negotiation and signing of the Korean Armistice in 1953 is an example of an incomplete negotiation - an incomplete (since Korea remained divided) negotiation but a negotiation that resulted in the Korean Armistice, nonetheless. As noted, Rhee refused to sign the Korean Armistice, and his demands to the United States were never met. For example, there was a disagreement between the United States and the Republic of Korea on reimbursements for the South Korean currency the Won sold to servicemen, the United States offered 63M and the ROK wanted 97M (Stokesbury, 1988).

Figure 7: UN delegate Lieut. Gen. William K. Harrison, Jr. (seated left), and Korean People's Army and Chinese People's Volunteers delegate, Gen. Nam Il (seated right) signing the Korean War armistice agreement at P'anmunjŏm, Korea, July 27, 1953. U.S. D

Following the Armistice agreement in 1954, the United States and United Nations were unable to get the communists to fully comply with the terms of the Armistice. United Nations sanctions were passed, and are in place indefinitely, but still, the communists refused and still refuse to have free elections in North Korea. The negotiations resulted in an Armistice agreement - yet without full compliance. Combat ended without reconciliation between North Korea and South Korea for 75 years - since the Soviet Union, Great Britain, and the USSR established the Joint Soviet-American Commission and divided Korea into North and South.

The US forces were gradually withdrawn, with a promise of economic development programs for the Republic of Korea. The United States was very concerned that the Republic of Korea, under Rhee, would unilaterally seek to militarily reunite Korea. All in all, the historical evidence demonstrates that Ike made a very deliberate and difficult decision in the Korean Conflict to avoid engagement in a much-escalated conflict with the North Koreans.

Ike was very enthusiastic about the post armistice rebuilding of South Korea. South Korea now has the 11th highest GDP in the world - right after Canada. South Korea has free and fair elections and has an aggregate freedom score from Freedom House of 83 out of 100, about the same as the United States. Whereas, North Korea has a freedom rating of 3 out of 100 This is part of Ike's legacy. However, there are still hardliners who argue that had Truman and Eisenhower taken the counsel of General MacArthur to fully pursue the communists in a widened war, the world may have rid itself of the totalitarian states in North Korea, China, and even Russia. This is possible, yet counterfactual. What if Rhee was right and the United States should have supported the reunification of Korea at all costs; we might now have an economic and democratic miracle in all of Korea.

Herbert Brownell, Ike's Attorney General from 1953 to 1957, had this to say about Ike and the Korean War, "It was interesting the way he ended the Korean War. Within a few weeks, after he had been elected, he went to Korea and he conferred with the generals there. General Mark Clark gave him a military plan for invading China and General Van Fleet gave him a plan for carrying on the war within the boundaries of Korea. He came back and decided that the public was unsupportive of a full-scale war in Korea, and he got out of it fast, which is an example of his decisive type of leadership" (Thompson, 1984, p. 170).

To employ strong negotiation, use all the resources and expertise that you have available in your negotiations (Ike used his Cabinet, the US JCS, and the US NSC). Be sure to examine ALL the options dispassionately. Ike had his staff repeatedly run through numerous possible scenarios for Korea. Ike had analysts do this over and over to examine all the possible outcomes. ALL options were on the table, including the nuclear option.

More than 2 million souls were lost in the Korean War. Most of the other options Ike had for the Korean War involved tens of thousands more lives being lost. This was a trade-off that Ike refused to make. Other American generals, including General Douglas MacArthur, believed otherwise. They believed that escalating the Korean War and the subsequent lives lost was a risk worth taking and a price worth paying for the potential defeat of North Korea, a Korean Unification, and the permanent defeat of Communist China. Imagine a counterfactual history where Communist China was defeated by the United States and Chiang Kai-shek became the leader of China. Perhaps all of Korea would have experienced the economic and political success of South Korea, and China would now be the world's largest capitalist country.

Lou Villaire

Chapter 3
The Suez Crisis of 1956: Leverage What You Have

Figure 8: Suez Troop Movement, Suez Canal 1956

President Eisenhower was angry. Three of the most loyal allies of the United States had deceived him. It was 1956 and Israel, France, and the United Kingdom had just invaded Egypt. The military invasion followed the Egyptian nationalization of the Suez Canal Company. In July of 1956, Colonel Gamal Abdel Nasser declared the international waterway (of which the UK owned 44%) the property of Egypt.

The Suez Crisis was also known as the Tripartite Aggression (UK, France, and Israel) and also as the Kadesh Operation. The purpose of the invasion was for France and Great Britain to regain control of the Suez Canal and to depose Egyptian President Gamal Abdel Nasser. The Suez Canal Company was jointly owned and operated by Great Britain and France. Nasser was an Egyptian nationalist and a populist who resented the colonial legacy of Great Britain and France owning, operating, and profiting from (at the expense of

Egypt and its people) the Suez Canal Company. The UK, France, and Israel military invasion plan was called MUSKETEER (Immerman, 1990).

Eisenhower was irate with Israel, France, and Great Britain because they undertook the invasion with no prior notice to the United States. Ike felt blindsided by these close allies. Eisenhower was very concerned about the rising tensions in the Middle East, and he was worried that Nasser's Egypt, as an emerging Middle East power, would embrace the Eastern Bloc Countries in return for military assistance from the Soviet Union. Eisenhower worried the situation would draw the Middle East into a broader conflict.

Nevertheless, Eisenhower's response to the invasion of Egypt seemed somewhat out of character. Ostensibly, Eisenhower claimed that this action against Egypt was a colonial power aggression against a sovereign nation. Yet the Suez Canal had been majority-owned and operated by France and Great Britain since its construction in 1869. Eisenhower used his considerable position and strong negotiation power to pressure Great Britain and France to accept a United Nations (UN) ceasefire. Eisenhower even went as far as to support a UN resolution condemning the invasion, along with the creation of a UN peacekeeping force in the region.

In the aftermath of the invasion and the subsequent withdrawal of the UK, French, and Israeli forces, the United States became the preeminent military power in the Middle East. The events of the Suez Crisis gave rise to what became known as the Eisenhower Doctrine. The Eisenhower Doctrine, which Eisenhower outlined to a joint session of the US Congress in January 1957, held that a sovereign Middle Eastern country could request American economic assistance or aid from US military forces if threatened by armed aggression. The Suez Crisis was one of the final stands for French and British colonialism. This is followed by a post-colonial power structure that placed the United States as the primary weapon supplier and protector to those Middle Eastern Nations which allied themselves with the United States rather than the USSR. The United States now supplies about half of all the weapons to the Middle East - with Saudi Arabia being the single largest recipient of US weapons shipments AND the single largest recipient of weapons in the world (Devine, 1981, p. 198).

Eisenhower broke forcefully with several of the most important United States allies. This was strong negotiation from Ike.

Figure 9: Suez Canal, Egypt, Circa 1956

It seemed that Eisenhower sided with Nasser and the newly established Egyptian Republic. Eisenhower was driven by a fear of the spread of Soviet Communism in the Middle East. Ike also sought US hegemony in the Middle East, along with a lucrative market for US weapons manufacturers.

Eisenhower did negotiate in good faith in the Suez Crisis. Eisenhower exercised his considerable power as a strong negotiator and furthered United States' interests in the Middle East. The Suez Crisis of 1956 had its origins in English Colonial rule in the Middle East. The Suez Canal was a tense issue for the Egyptians since its construction in 1869. To understand the Suez Crisis, it is essential to put it in the long-term context of Middle East and North African Colonialism.

The Suez Canal was built in partnership with the French and financed by European banks. During the construction of the Suez Canal, there were large sums of money that went to patronage and corruption. New taxes that helped fund the Suez Canal caused popular discontent among the Egyptian people. In 1875 the Egyptian *Khedive* (Viceroy) Isma'il Pasha avoided national bankruptcy by selling all Egypt's shares in the Suez Canal to the British government. The sale of Egyptian shares in the Suez Canal resulted in the imposition of British and French controllers in the Egyptian cabinet. Thus, the real power in the Egyptian cabinet were the French and English bondholders of the Suez Canal Company.

The Egyptian Muhammad Ali Dynasty became a British client. Isma'il and Tewfik Pasha governed Egypt as a quasi-independent state as an Ottoman suzerain until the British military incursion and occupation of 1882. Local anger with Isma'il Pasha and British occupation brought about the first Egyptian nationalist groups in 1879. Ahmad Urabi was a prominent figure in these nationalist groups. Fearing a loss of their colonial control, the UK and France intervened militarily, bombarding Alexandria and stopping Egyptian dissent. As Ike put it in his 1963 memoirs: "British forces first entered Egypt on July 10, 1882. Under the Constantinople Convention of 1888 - signed by Britain,

Austria-Hungary, France, Germany, Holland, Italy, Russia, Spain, Turkey - the Canal was to remain open in times of both war and peace to every vessel of commerce or of war" (Eisenhower, 1963, p. 195).

By the time of the Battle of Tel El Kebir in 1882, 80% of all shipping along the Suez Canal was British vessels, most of it between India and Britain. The Suez Canal facilitated the exercise of the power and the colonial reach of the world's strongest naval force - the British Navy. The Battle of Tel El Kebir was fought between the Egyptian army led by Ahmed Urabi and the British military of Garnet Wolseley, near Tel El Kebir. After discontented Egyptian officers under Urabi rebelled in 1882, the United Kingdom reacted to protect its interests in the country, especially the Suez Canal.

The Battle of Tel El Kebir was a long-lasting defeat for the Egyptians. The official British numbers listed a total of 57 British troops killed. Two thousand Egyptians were killed by British forces. Power was then given back to the *Khedive*. The *Khedivate* of Egypt was an Ottoman province until November of 1914 when it was declared a British protectorate. The establishment of Egypt as a British protectorate was the direct result of the decision of the Young Turks of the Ottoman Empire to join World War I on the side of the Central Powers (Austria-Hungary, Germany, Bulgaria, and the Ottoman Empire).

After World War I, Saad Zaghlul and the Wafd Party led the Egyptian nationalist movement to a majority at the local Legislative Assembly. Zaghlul presented the case for Egyptian independence to the British High Commissioner in hopes that the Commissioner would allow the representatives to bring the case for Egyptian independence to the Paris Peace Conference. The British High Commissioner (Sir Reginald Wingate) promptly denied the request, after which the British exiled Zaghlul and his associates to the Island of Malta (at that time a British Colony) in March of 1919. The people of Egypt then rose up in their first modern revolution. After weeks of nationwide violence resulting in hundreds of Egyptians killed and injured, the British Commissioner relented. Zaghlul was allowed to return to Egypt from exile and then to lead a delegation to Paris in April of 1919. At this time, British Prime Minister David Lloyd George convinced France and the United States that the question of Egyptian independence was an imperial rather than an international question. And in a blow to the Egyptian nationalists, the day they arrived in Paris, US President Woodrow Wilson recognized Britain's protectorate over Egypt. The Egyptian nationalist delegates never even received a formal hearing at the Paris Peace Conference. Because of the growing nationalism following the Egyptian people's revolt, The Egyptian people's revolt of 1918 eventually led the UK to issue a unilateral declaration of Egypt's independence four years later in February of 1922. The UK dissolved the protectorate and established the Independent Kingdom of Egypt. Sarwat Pasha became the Egyptian Prime Minister.

WWI and its aftermath had a profound impact on the Middle East. As the 400 plus year, Ottoman Empire fell it was replaced by European imperialism. Article 22 of the Covenant of the League of Nations (established in the aftermath of WWI) put in place the Mandate System. The Mandate System subdivided the Middle East and West and Central Africa as well as Southwest Africa into de-facto European colonies. After 400 years of unified Ottoman Muslim rule in the Middle East, the Arabs and the land in the Middle East were divided into several smaller states that were dominated by British and French imperial rule. Throughout WWI, the imperial powers devised various means of subdividing the Middle East - anticipating the spoils of war.

Nations that were created after WWI, such as Lebanon, Syria, and Iraq, have since experienced a great deal of division. Indeed, before the colonial powers partitioning the Middle East, the area of Syria encompassed the nations of Syria, Lebanon, Israel, Palestine, and Jordan. Since this time, Egyptian nationalism has been a very powerful force and continues as the dominant force in Egyptian politics. After WWI and WWII, and until the 1952 Egyptian nationalist revolution, Egypt was controlled (answerable to the British Monarchy) by an elite class made up of interrelated families of Turkish, Circassian, and Albanian origin known to historians as the Turco-Circassian elite who owned most of the land of Egypt - which the *fellaheen* (Egyptian peasants) worked as tenant farmers. In a display and practice of extraordinary inequality and servitude, the Turco-Circassian aristocracy made up less than 1% of the Egyptian population but owned 3/4 of all the farmland in Egypt.

The Egyptian Revolution of 1952 (also known as the 1952 Coup d'état or the July 23 Revolution), began on July 23, 1952, by the Egyptian Free Officers Movement, a group of army officers led by Mohammed Naguib and Gamal Abdel Nasser. The revolution was aimed at overthrowing King Farouk I. General Nasser (a rising nationalist star in the Egyptian military) overthrew King Farouk I, who was modestly known to himself as 'His Majesty Farouk I, by the grace of God, King of Egypt and Sudan, Sovereign of Nubia, Kordofan, and of Darfur.'

Nasser quickly sought to abolish the British constitutional monarchy and throw out the aristocracy of Egypt and Sudan. Nasser sought to establish an Egyptian Republic and to end the British occupation of Egypt. Nasser also sought the independence of Sudan (previously governed as an Anglo-Egyptian condominium). The Nasser government sought international non-alignment with either the communists in the East or the capitalists in the West. Nasser's popularity in Egypt and the Arab world skyrocketed after he nationalized the Suez Canal and his political victory in the subsequent Suez Crisis. Eisenhower considered Nasser somewhat untrustworthy. However, Eisenhower had respect for Nasser and the self-determination of the Arab people that Nasser embodied. Nasser had strong political instincts, was a political opportunist, and referred to himself as a tactical neutralist of the non-aligned nation movement. (Kissinger, 2012).

Figure 10: Eisenhower and Gamal Abdel Nasser, Cir 1956.

Nasser was reviled by the UK, France, and Israel. By 1955 Nasser was importing arms from the Soviet Bloc and was using those weapons to arm the *fedayeen* (one who sacrifices himself), the Sons of Pharaoh, and the Sons of Islam to undertake raids of Israel to 'cleanse the land of Palestine.' Nasser's Arab nationalism (and Arab Nationalism to this day) viewed Israel as an illegitimate occupying power in the Middle East. Nasser directly supported attacks on Israel with the exiled Palestinian leader Hajj Amin al-Husseini, the *mufti* of Jerusalem. Amin al-Husseini was exiled in Cairo at the time (Doran, 2016, p. 143).

France and England wanted the United States, as their main ally, to support them in their efforts to remove Nasser from power. Yet Eisenhower refused to support them in their military opposition to Nasser. Ike asked, "What is the endpoint? How do you bring this to a conclusion?" Ike's stated view was that the Suez Canal Company operated in the territory of Egypt; and that Egypt had the authority to nationalize the Canal if there was fair compensation to the Canal shareholders - namely France and the UK. Ike also expected Egypt to honor the Charter of the Canal and keep it open to international traffic. Ike was careful to recognize Egyptian sovereignty without damaging the rights of others. But according to the UK, the nationalization of the Canal was a violation of the Suez Treaty. The UK and France claimed that Egypt was unable to operate the canal. Egypt successfully nationalized the Suez Canal and ultimately provided monetary compensation to the shareholders for their losses.

Nasser also resented France for supplying arms to Israel. Nasser was driven by the Arab defeat in the 1948 war with Israel, and he was vehemently opposed to the formation of the Jewish State in the Middle East. The United States sought reconciliation between Israel and Egypt and offered the funds to construct the Aswan Dam. Israel and Egypt were at odds in significant ways - including the demand on the part of Nasser that Israel give up the southern desert region of the Negev (which constituted more than half of the territory of Israel) along with hundreds of thousands of Palestinian refugees being given the right to repatriate to Palestine (Kissinger, 2012).

Initially, the United States was going to supply the money and the technical expertise for Nasser and Egypt to build the Aswan Dam in the Nile River Valley. Secretary of State John Foster Dulles and President Eisenhower also agreed to supply Nasser with US military aid, but the US military aid was for defensive purposes only and under the supervision of US military advisors. Nasser rejected these conditions and turned to the USSR for aid to build the Aswan Dam.

On the United States' side, US Senators representing Southern states objected to the United States funding of the Aswan Dam because it would result in much more cotton being grown in Egypt. That would, in turn, reduce the value of US cotton on the world market. The United States notified Egypt of its intention to withdraw its support for funding of the Aswan Dam and within a week Nasser had nationalized the Suez Canal Corporation. When Nasser announced the nationalization of the Suez Canal, he spoke to a crowd of 100,000 in Liberation Square in Alexandria, informing the crowd that the tolls from the Canal would now go to the Egyptian nation's building of the Aswan Dam (Devine, 1981, p. 81).

"We shall industrialize Egypt and compete with the West." Nasser's ardent nationalism had established greater unity among the Arab States and greater enmity toward Israel along with sporadic attacks on Israel. "At this moment as I talk to you, some of your Egyptian brethren have started to take over the canal company and its property and to control shipping in the canal - the canal which is situated in Egyptian

In Good Faith

territory, which is part of Egypt and which is owned by Egypt" (Devine, 1981).

Immediately after the speech by Nasser, the English Prime Minister, Anthony Eden, cabled Eisenhower and stated, "If we do not take a firm stand, our influence and yours throughout the Middle East will, we are convinced, be finally destroyed" (Kissinger, 2012, p. 531). Several days later, Eden went in front of the English House of Commons and stated that an arrangement that left the Suez Canal in the power of a single nation would be rejected by Her Majesty's government. US Secretary of State Dulles favored bringing public opinion around to support the international operation of the Canal. Ike and US representatives had a long-term postcolonial view and recognized the opportunity for the United States to become a dominant Middle East power following the collapse of European colonialism. The Great Powers were on their way out and the United States (or the USSR) was on its way in.

To mitigate the damage being done to the long-standing allied relationship that the United States had with France and the UK, the United States framed the Suez Canal dispute as a legal one rather than an existential one. Immediately after the nationalization of the Suez by Egypt, Ike sent Eden a letter which stated the "unwisdom of even contemplating the use of military force at this moment" (Letter from Eisenhower to UK Prime Minister Eden, July 1956). Ike seemed convinced that the UK and France would avoid military action without the support of the United States.

However, according to a sharp analysis of the Suez Crisis by Henry Kissinger, "as it happened, moral pressure proved insufficient in precisely the same proportion to which physical force had been ruled out" (Kissinger, p. 536). In fact, an insightful reporter asked Dulles at a September 13,

1956 press conference, "Mr. Secretary, with the United States announcing it will not use force, and with Soviet Russia backing Egypt with its propaganda, does that not leave all the trump cards in Mr. Nasser's hands" (Kissinger, 2012, p. 539)? Dulles seemed to believe that moral force would prevail in the Suez Crisis. Ike had a pragmatic and long-range view of the Suez Canal Crisis. Privately Ike thought the nationalization of the Suez Canal was a bad move on Nasser's part. Ike also believed that the United States' use of force against Nasser would "array the Muslim world from Dakur to the Philippines against us" (Memorandum of a Conference-With the President, White House, Washington, D.C. 1956).

Nasser was very shrewd in his use of the capitalist West and the communist East to bargain for what Egypt wanted. Both the USSR and the United States were willing to provide Nasser with military and economic support in return for strengthening their position in the Middle East. The more Nasser moved toward the Soviets, the more the United States reached out to Nasser with benefits and vice versa. The older colonial and Great Power alignments were giving way to newer geopolitical alignments in which the United States was defining its strategic interests in a very different way than its European allies. The United States was free of the burden of a colonial past in the Middle East, and the US military was much stronger than France, the UK, or Israel.

This approach by Ike also included separating the ownership of the Canal from its operations. As Ike had noted several times, the Egyptians were within their rights to nationalize the Canal, if the current owners were compensated for their lost financial interests. Ike had a distrustful view of Nasser, but Ike could separate the problem of traffic on the Suez Canal from the personality of Nasser. Ike recognized the history of European colonialism as a brutal history that had long denied the sovereign rights of the Egyptian people.

Ike describes his negotiating style in his memoir *Mandate for Change*, "I have always deplored and deprecated table-pounding and name-calling; such methods I have long believed, are normally self-defeating defense mechanisms. On the world scene, practiced by governments, such mechanisms are tragically stupid and ultimately worthless" (Eisenhower, 1963, p 193). Ike goes on in his memoirs to describe his approach to negotiation: "To be effective in the nation's rightful role as a Free World leader, our people and their government should always, in my view, display a spirit of firmness without truculence, conciliation without appeasement, confidence without arrogance" (Eisenhower, 1963, p. 193). And in one more piece of guidance on negotiating from Ike, "Ultimate objectives must be paramount; immediate reactions are less important." It did not seem that there was an ultimate objective of the United States in the Middle East.

The British and the French were initially patient with the United States in attempts by Ike and Dulles to resolve the Suez Canal dispute including engaging in the Maritime Conference and the Users Association and then the Six Principles: "(1) There should be free and open transit through the Canal without discrimination, overt or covert – this covers both political and technical aspects. (2) The sovereignty of Egypt should be respected. (3) The operation of the Canal should be insulated from the politics of any country. (4) The manner of fixing tolls and charges should be decided by agreement between Egypt and the users. (5) A fair proportion of the dues should be allotted to development. (6) In case of disputes, unresolved affairs between the Suez Canal Company and the Egyptian government should be settled by arbitration with suitable terms of reference and suitable provisions for the payment of sums found to be due" (United Nations, 1956).

Ike stated in a 1956 news conference that the means for the dispute resolution in the 1950 Tripartite Agreement was one the parties had agreed they would use reasonable methods to prevent hostilities (Eisenhower, 1956). Once again Eisenhower used a strategy of enlarging a problem in order to help solve it. Ike considered the Nasser Canal seizure as more than a UK and French problem. Ike wrote Anthony Eden, "The maximum number of maritime nations affected by the Nasser action should be consulted quickly in the hope of obtaining an agreed basis of understanding." (widening the problem) In his analysis, Ike is calm, dispassionate, and amoral.

It was in October of 1956 that France and the UK entered into a secret agreement with Israel to attack Egypt. On the October 29, 1956, Israel would mount a surprise attack on the Sinai aimed at the Gaza Strip. Pretending surprise, France and the UK would then demand on October 30, 1956 that both Egypt and Israel withdraw within 12 hours from the area of the Suez Canal. With Egypt expected to refuse, the French and the Brits would send troops to protect the Suez Canal. The leaders of both France and the UK expected that the United States would accept their actions as a *fait accompli*. Ike surprised the French and the UK by strongly honoring the Tripartite Declaration of 1950, which opposed aggression between Israel and her neighbors. Furthermore, the United States would seek an immediate ceasefire through the United Nations (Devine, 1981).

When Ike heard of the invasion he stated, "Bombs, by God! What does Anthony (Eden) think he is doing" (Devine, 1981, p. 85)? Ike told his speechwriter Emmet Hughes that this attack was "the damnedest business I ever saw

In Good Faith

supposedly intelligent governments get themselves into." Later in a speech on October 31, 1956 Ike is quoted about the Suez Crisis "there can be no peace - without law" (Hughes, 1963, p 322).

In the meetings with Nasser and Deputy Under Secretary of State Loy Henderson from the US, Nasser stated that he would stand up to the UK. The UK Prime Minister Anthony Eden stated (who would later have a nervous breakdown related to the Suez Crisis) that the UK could not remain static. Nasser rejected the 18-Nation UN proposals for a truce and stayed firm with his demands. Nasser's position was one of immovable resistance. Nasser was resolute and ultimately accepted nothing but Egyptian control of the Suez Canal.

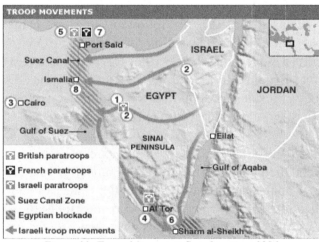

Figure 11: Troop Movements Suez Invasion, 1956.

French foreign minister Christian Pineau stated that the United States had refused any Egyptian sanctions and that the United States had "turned down all positive suggestions." The French and the Brits claimed that it was the inability of the United States to agree on any sanctions that forced the French, UK, and Israeli military action. The French ambassador to Moscow, Maurice Dejean, communicated that the USSR was telling Nasser to be unyielding because the UK and France were bluffing in their military threats. Most other world nations supported Egyptian sovereignty over French and UK colonialism. The UK stated that because the United States wanted all the Suez Canal tolls to go to Egypt, Egypt lacked an incentive to negotiate.

According to Nasser, the nationalization of the Suez Canal in secret was necessary otherwise France and the UK would have moved in to prevent the action. The French demanded that Egypt accept international operation of the Canal, while Nasser continued to block any "measure of international operation." In order to apply financial pressure, the UK blocked Egyptian monies in London. In a top-secret memo only released in 1999, the following message came from Nasser to the United States on October 31, 1956: "Nasser intends to request that the US offer Egypt military assistance if Great Britain and France invade. Nasser wishes urgently to know President Eisenhower's reaction. He is not asking for Russian help, at least for the present."

Prior to the attack, there was an extensive conversation between the United States, the UK, France, Egypt, and other Suez Canal user nations about the international legal implications of the Suez Canal and the rights of all user nations to use the Canal. This was done in the hope of avoiding the invasion and establishing an international regulatory body that would run the Canal. These attempts at negotiation obviously failed to prevent the attack. Ike repeatedly warned Prime Minister Eden that undertaking the attack was a very bad move and would result in negative consequences all around. "I really do not see how a successful resolution could be achieved by forcible means.

In Good Faith

The use of force, would, it seems to me, vastly increase the area of jeopardy." Ike communicated privately that the United States was willing to consider military action if Nasser closed the Canal illegally and refused to reopen it stating, "the fate of Western Europe must never be placed at the whim of a dictator." However, under the present circumstances, Ike held that the crisis should be resolved with self-restraint and negotiation (Eisenhower, 1965).

On October 29, Israel invaded the Egyptian Sinai and the United States stayed out. The USSR stated that they would intervene to help Egypt. The United States replied to the USSR "you do, and we will respond." Shortly after the attack, Egypt sank the ship, Akka, in the Suez Canal to block shipping traffic. Egypt said it was done by UK and French aircraft, but the ship was loaded with rocks and cement before it was sunk, specifically to block passage through the Suez Canal. During the midst of the crisis, Ike went on US national television on October 31, 1956 to tell the people of the United States, "As it is the manifest right of any of these nations to take such decisions and actions, it is likewise our right - if our judgment so dictates - to dissent. We believe these actions to have been taken in error. For we do not accept the use of force as a wise and proper instrument for the settlement of international disputes."

On November 1, 1956, Ike wrote to John Foster Dulles that the first objective of the United Nations in the Suez Crisis should be to achieve a ceasefire because this will: " (a) keep the war from spreading, and (b) give me time to find out what each side is trying to gain, and (c), to develop a final resolution that will represent the considered judgment of the United Nations respecting past blame and future action" (Eisenhower et al. 2002, p. 2037). Ike went on to write to Dulles; "Unilateral actions now taken by the United States must *not* single out and condemn *any one nation* - but should serve to emphasize to the world our hope for a quick cease-fire to be followed by sane and deliberate action on the part of the United Nations, resulting, hopefully, in a solution to which all parties would adhere by each conceding something" (Eisenhower et al. 2001, p. 2057). Here Ike displays his quick, forceful, and insightful analysis of the situation, with a direct aim to negotiate a solution.

Figure 12: Eisenhower and US Secretary of State, John Foster Dulles, 1956.

Dulles was persistent in his high-minded claims that both France and the UK had violated Article 1 of the NATO Treaty by using force in the Suez Crisis. Dulles contended that the NATO Treaty Article 1 "...requires all the parties to that treaty to renounce the use of force and to settle their disputes by peaceful means. That is our complaint: that the treaty was violated; not that there was no consultation" (Nichols 2011, p. 271). In a meeting in the US presidential cabinet room on October 29, 1956, just after the attack commenced, Ike fumed about the invasion. Ike conceded that the UK had reasons for being at odds with Nasser, but none of those reasons justified a military invasion, and "nothing justifies double-crossing us (the US).

Further, during a meeting with Arthur Flemming, the US director of defense mobilization, Ike held forth on the effect that the invasion would have on world oil supplies. Ike predicted that the French and Brits would soon have difficulty with their own oil supplies and that they would be "short of dollars to finance these operations." And to make a bad situation worse for the Brits, the Syrians had destroyed three pipelines that carried oil from Kirkuk in Iraq to the Mediterranean for shipment to Europe. Ike viewed the situation as one in which the United States would have to decide between long-standing allies and the rule of law. "We cannot proclaim this integrity when the issue is easy - and stifle it when the issue is hard" (Hitchcock, 2018, pp. 325, 326).

The fidelity that Ike had to the *rule of law* in the Middle East was accurate yet dubious considering that just three years earlier the CIA, under the direction of Ike, had orchestrated a *coup d'etat* in Iran along with the UK (Churchill), code-named Operation Ajax to depose the democratically elected government of Prime Minister Mohammad Mossadegh. The United States undertook this criminal action because the Mossadegh government had seized the operations of British Petroleum (BP) and Ike believed that the Mossadegh government was quickly moving towards Soviet Communism. The United States restored the monarch Mohammad Reza Shah to the *Peacock Throne*. The Shah was a brutal dictator who ruled for almost forty years, murdering his political enemies.

UK Prime Minister Eden was evidently receiving covert information directly from an operative within the Nasser government. The intelligence that Eden was receiving from the source may have been intentional misinformation as Eden was operating under wrong information. Or possibly, Eden had some other motivation to think that the Egyptian people considered Nasser a tyrant and thus would welcome the UK and French soldiers as liberators. Perhaps a few of the Egyptian people viewed Nasser unfavorably, but the overwhelming majority of Egyptians supported Nasser and his nationalization of the Suez Canal. And the invasion of Egypt further united the Egyptian people behind Nasser in the face of a common foe. Egyptians celebrated the nationalization of the Suez Canal. As a result of the nationalization of the Suez Canal and the revenues that flowed to Egypt from the canal fees, along with the subsequent construction of the Aswan Dam, the quality of life for most Egyptians improved.

Immediately following the attack, the United States went to the United Nations General Assembly to condemn the attack and attempt to end the invasion. The United States communicated to Israel that unless Israel desisted with the occupation, the United States would impose sanctions on Israel. In a record of decision, immediately after the Israeli invasion, the United States stated that it would suspend development assistance to Israel, suspend technical assistance, surplus agricultural products would be suspended, investment guarantees would be terminated, and the United States would delay Israeli imports. These were heavy sanctions on the part of the United States towards its ally, Israel.

Shortly after the attack, on November 9, 1956, the Israeli leader Ben-Gurion agreed to withdraw Israeli troops from the Sinai. By November 5, UN peacekeeping forces were put in place, and France and the UK declared that their forces would be removed forthwith. The UK ordered a ceasefire on November 6, 1956. Ike commented that he had pushed for a negotiated peace ever since Nasser had seized the Canal on July 26, 1956. Ike stated that nothing justified the actions that Israel, the UK, and France took, and that Egypt had the legal right to nationalize the Canal (Devine 1981). Ike stated: "The real point is that Britain, France, and Israel had come to believe - probably correctly - that Nasser was their worst enemy in the Mideast and that until he was removed or defeated, they would have no peace. I do not quarrel with the idea that there is justification for such fears, but I have insisted long and earnestly that you cannot resort to force in international relationships because of your fear of what might happen in the future" (Eisenhower, 2021, p. 165).

Ike believed that this action was an opportunity handed to the Russians. He communicated passionately to Anthony Eden that he refused to use force in the Suez crisis. Then Eden went 'silent' before the invasion. Ike stated that he failed to see the benefit in a scheme that would "antagonize the entire Muslim world." The United States kept up the pressure on the UK to remove the British troops as soon as possible. The United States even blocked the repatriation of dollars Britain had supplied to the International Monetary Fund (IMF). On November 12, 1956, British Prime Minister Eden told the cabinet that the UK dollar reserves were very low and that if the situation went unresolved, the UK would be forced to devalue its currency. Even though Eden assured Ike that the Suez Tripartite Aggression was "not part of harking back to old colonial and occupational concepts," Ike remained unconvinced.

Ike had several strong tools at hand - international pressure (the United Nations and Suez Canal users), monetary policy (US and international), economic sanctions (UK, France, and Israel), moral and legal arguments (the rule of law and non-intervention). In his analysis of the Suez Crisis, Kissinger asks whether the United States had such a stark choice between providing the UK and France full support in their invasion or opposing it vehemently altogether. To the Egyptians, this was a story that had played out before in 1882 when the British imperialists attacked to protect their ill-gotten interests in the Suez Canal. Kissinger goes on to perceptively claim that the United States put forward three principles in the Suez Crisis: (1) the commitments that the United States had towards its allies were tempered by legal concerns; (2) military intervention was only justified in the face of pure self-defense; and (3) the United States really wanted to pursue its own interests and become a leader in the Middle East. In an even more proscribed view, Kissinger goes on to communicate "diplomacy involves, at least in part, the ability to discriminate among cases and to distinguish friends from opponents." Maybe Ike would have called this existential view by Kissinger situational ethics or amorality, or simply diplomacy?

One of the factors that contributed to a relatively quick ceasefire on the part of the UK was the fact that there was a sharp decline in the UK's dollar reserves, which coincidentally, the United States declined to stem. Oil exports had come to a virtual halt - with the UK and France getting 75% of their petroleum via the Suez Canal. And the United States refused to provide any oil supply assistance to the UK or France until they removed their forces from Egypt. This was a coercive maneuver on the part of the United States. Ike used the full force of US economic and diplomatic power to reverse the invasion (Devine, 1981). On November 22, 1956, the UK's Harold MacMillan, Chancellor of the Exchequer (and successor to Eden as the UK PM), told the United States that the UK would start the withdrawal of its troops from Egypt. Then on December 2, 1956, the UK told the United States that the UK and French troops would be withdrawn from the Suez in 15 days.

In Good Faith

Negotiating requests that the United States made of Egypt after the invasion were that Egypt would curtail its relationship with the USSR, recognize its obligations under international law, respect the armistice agreement with Israel, and oppose anti-western propaganda. Furthermore, the armistice required Egypt to accept the payment of tolls on the Suez Canal by a neutral agency, that only 50% of the tolls would go to Egypt, and that Egypt would operate the Canal in accordance with accepted principles. Finally, the ceasefire required Egypt to clear the Canal of debris and to cease any more *fedayeen* raids into Israel. On November 4, 1956, Israel respected the United Nations' request for a ceasefire and stopped its operations in the Sinai. But Israel had already achieved their goals. They took control of Gaza and lifted the blockade at the Gulf of Aqaba. The French and the Brits were unsuccessful, and the Egyptian military fought hard denying France and the UK control of the Suez Canal.

After the ceasefire, Ike continued to seek sanctions on Israel, but both the Senate Majority Leader, Lyndon Johnson, and the Senate Minority Leader, William Knowland, opposed the sanctions. However, Ike persisted and eventually persuaded Israel to respect the UN Declaration and allow for UN peacekeeping forces to occupy Gaza and the Sinai. Suez Canal traffic resumed on March 6, 1957. The Israeli withdrawal of its troops prevented a showdown between the executive branch and Congress (Ike and the US Senate). Ike felt very strongly that there should be consequences for the invasion of Gaza and Sinai by Israel.

There were really no winners in the Suez Crisis, although Egypt did win control of the Suez Canal. In the negotiated truce at the Suez Canal, all sides had to engage in concessions. If there was any winner, it was Ike and the United States, since the United States became the dominant military force in the Middle East. And US oil companies would continue to control a larger and larger share of the Middle East oil until the formation of OPEC. Indeed, Ike used the Eisenhower Doctrine in 1957 to support King Hussein in Jordan. There was a nationalist threat to the throne of King Hussein. Ike, with Congressional funding, moved the Sixth US Fleet in support of Hussein, and the display of US force succeeded in protecting the King (Devine, 1981, p. 96). Nasser continued his Arab Nationalism, and he and his allies had a hard time admitting that the opposition by the United States to the French, Israeli, and UK invasion was what prevented a prolonged war. At the same time, the United States failed to improve its standing with the 'non-aligned' nations in the world as a result of the tacit United States support of Egyptian self-determination (Kissinger, 2012).

Ike and Dulles believed that it was both the legacy of British and French colonialism and Nasser's arrogance and belligerence that were to blame for the Suez Crisis. Yet, this position does seem to sidestep the fact that the United States used the Suez Crisis to put itself in a dominant position of power in the Middle East. This was the politics of expediency. Indeed, Ike and Dulles had discussed in private the possibility of the United States using a covert operation (like Iran and Guatemala) to remove Nasser from power. Ironically, Dulles later stated, "if the aggression were allowed to stand, we would have, I fear torn this (UN) charter into shreds and the world would again be in a world of anarchy" (Immerman, 1990, p. 154).

It was on January 5, 1957 that Ike addressed a joint session of the US Congress to announce what became known as the Eisenhower Doctrine. In this "Special Message to the Congress on the Situation in the Middle East," it was proclaimed by Eisenhower that a Middle Eastern country could request American economic assistance or aid from US military forces if it was being threatened by armed aggression. Eisenhower singled out the USSR threat in his doctrine by authorizing the commitment of US forces "to secure and protect the territorial integrity and political independence of such nations, requesting such aid against overt armed aggression from any nation controlled by international communism." The phrase "international communism" made the doctrine much broader than simply responding to Soviet military action. A danger that might be linked to communists of any nation could conceivably invoke the doctrine (Hitchcock, 2018, p. 339).

One of the main and most effective pressure points that Ike had to coerce was that of financial pressure. The Bank of England had lost 45 million dollars between October 30 and November 2, 1956 and the supply of oil to Britain had been very restricted by the closing of the Suez Canal. Subsequently, the UK sought immediate relief from the International Monetary Fund (IMF). The assistance was denied by the United States. Ike even instructed the Secretary of the US Treasury, George M. Humphrey, to get ready to sell part of the US British Sterling bond holdings. The UK Chancellor of the Exchequer, Harold Macmillan, communicated to Anthony Eden that the United States was prepared to follow through on this threat. Macmillan further communicated to Eden that the UK would suffer tremendously with the devaluation of the British Pound. These warnings on the part of Macmillan may have been overstated in order to help force Eden from the Prime Ministership. Regardless, the financial coercion on the part of the United States towards the UK was real and had a very damaging effect on Eden and his administration. Under duress, Eden made a quick capitulation to the United States and international demands for a ceasefire in the Suez Crisis (Kissinger, 2012).

Immediately following the UK, French, and Israeli invasion of Egypt, Saudi Arabia, in coordination with the United States, put in place an oil embargo against the UK and France. The United States also refused to supply the two countries with any oil until the UK and France agreed to a troop removal from the Suez. Other oil producers members also agreed not to sell any oil to the UK or France. This was more coercion on the part of Ike. In the Suez Crisis, Ike quickly created control, and he was expedient in responding to the Crisis.

In his entreaty to Congress for the Eisenhower Doctrine, Ike announced: "First, America's vital interests are worldwide, embracing both hemispheres and every continent. Second, we have a community of interest with every nation in the free world. Third, the interdependence of interests requires a decent respect for the rights and the peace of all peoples" (Halford, 1993, p. 169).

As a result of the geopolitical situation in the Middle East at the time, and in particular the Suez Crisis, the Eisenhower Doctrine emerged. The Eisenhower Doctrine was a three-part grant of authority to the US president in the Middle East: a 200-million-dollar grant to preserve the individual nation autonomy (prevent USSR influence) in the Middle East; military aid for these nations; and, permission for the president to use military action to protect these nations. A doctrine that has now persisted for successive US presidents for more than half a century, including US military interventions and occupations in Afghanistan, Iraq, Iran, Syria, and Palestine. This is in addition to the United States supplying billions of dollars in weapons to numerous Middle East countries including Saudi Arabia, the United Arab Emirates, and Israel (Devine, 1981).

Ike recognized the long game (1st, 2nd, and 3rd effects) and took advantage of the power vacuum left from the Middle East exit of the Great Powers for US ascendancy in the Middle East. More than 60 years later, we have some appreciation for the numerous United States Middle East military entanglements that have ensued. Millions of lives have been lost in wars in the Middle East since the Suez Crisis of 1956. The Eisenhower Doctrine, in its simpler form, has probably outlived its purpose. The United States is slowly unwinding its long-term, over-wielding presence in the Middle East, resulting in the shift for sovereign Middle East member states to fully exercise their own power.

Lou Villaire

Chapter 4
The Civil Rights Act (CRA) of 1957: Negotiate with Conscience and Guile

How Eisenhower used the strong desires of others and worked behind the scenes to pass the civil rights bill of 1957

Figure 13: Protest for Civil Rights, 1957.

By the US presidential election of 1956, less than 2 million African Americans were registered to vote out of a voting-age population of nine million nationwide. In Mississippi in 1956, only 7,000 African Americans out of an adult African American population of 500,000 were allowed to vote because of Jim Crow laws. Jim Crow laws were state and local laws that enforced racial segregation in the Southern United States. Jim Crow laws were passed in the late 1800s and the early 1900s by Democratic Party dominated state legislatures to prevent African Americans from voting. There was a strong Republican Party drive to pass legislation in the US Congress ensuring federal protection of the right to vote, specifically for blacks in the segregationist South. Southern Segregationist senators had successfully blocked any legislation to protect the right to vote. Eisenhower and his US Attorney General (AG), Herbert Brownell, were very much in support of enacting right to vote legislation in the US Congress (Eisenhower, 1957). Ike, Brownell, and their allies were determined to get the legislation enacted into law.

The Civil Rights Act (CRA) of 1957 became possible with a new mid-century congressional coalition of progressive Democrats and progressive Republicans. Lyndon Baines Johnson (LBJ), the Majority Leader in the US Senate (1955-1960), indicated that he was willing to allow the CRA to get to the Senate floor. Eisenhower communicated that he wanted a moderate bill "that would preserve rights without disturbing the rights of others." Southern opposition to the 1957 CRA claimed that the CRA would allow the president to use US troops in the South and deny the constitutional right of trial by jury to Southern whites who were accused of violating the voting rights of blacks (Nichols, 2007).

In the 1952 presidential election, Eisenhower received about 25% of the African American vote, and in 1956 he received about 40% of the African American vote. The Republican party was the predominant political party of African Americans for more than half a century after the presidency of Abraham Lincoln, up until President Franklin Delano Roosevelt's New Deal. At which time, African Americans became more in favor of the Democratic Party, in good part because of the job creation programs of the New Deal.

According to Ike (1965), the civil rights issue mattered to him and his administration because of moral and social conviction. Ike increased his share of the African American vote among voting populations in the North and South. Ike campaigned in 1952 on protecting the right to vote. Ike's advisors pushed him to pursue legislation that strengthened the American voting franchise based on race.

The 1952 Republican Party Platform included the following in its section on civil rights, "We believe that it is the primary responsibility of each state to order and control its own domestic institutions, and this power, reserved to the States, is essential to the maintenance of our Federal Republic. However, we believe that the Federal Government should take supplemental action within its constitutional jurisdiction to oppose discrimination against race, religion, or national origin." The 1952 Republican Party Platform went on to state, "We will prove our good faith by federal action toward the elimination of lynching and federal action toward the elimination of poll taxes as a prerequisite of voting" (US White House, December 8, 1955, pp. 43, 249). A Republican Party platform that included anti-lynching and anti-Jim Crow laws language was significant. According to the Tuskegee Institute, from the late 1800s to the 1950s, there were more than 4,000 lynching's of African Americans in the US Reconstruction States.

The 1956 Republican Party Convention was held at the Cow Palace in San Francisco from August 20 to 23. Before the Convention, a Republican Party civil rights Subcommittee and the US Justice Department sought to persuade Ike to take a strong position on civil rights during the Convention. The Subcommittee and the Justice Dept wanted an aggressive and unified statement on civil rights for negroes. Ike refused. The Justice Department under Brownell had a strong legislative program planned for civil rights and repeatedly pressed Ike to publicly adopt the program. Ike refused. Ultimately, the Republican Party civil rights Subcommittee stated publicly, "We support the enactment of the civil rights program already presented by the president to the Second Session of the 84th Congress" (Eisenhower, 1956, p. 172). This statement said little because Ike understood that all that had been presented to the 84th Congress thus far was to establish an Assistant Attorney General of Civil Rights in the Justice Department and to establish a Civil Rights Commission.

The response from the press was tepid, carrying reports that there was a program in the 1956 Republican Party platform for civil rights, although the program lacked specificity. The platform stated, "...the Republican Party accepts the decision of the US Supreme Court that racial discrimination in publicly supported schools must be progressively eliminated" (1956 US Republican Party Platform, p. 60). Ike continued, in his Convention speech and on the campaign trail, to take a narrow view on civil rights whereby he communicated that the case of civil rights for negroes in his administration was limited to direct federal jurisdiction - what the administration had the legal authority to do without violating states' rights.

However, Vice-President Nixon went further in his remarks at the Convention, "...equal opportunity to obtain proper housing, decent medical care, good education, and the unlimited chance for employment, according to his ability, which is every American's right" (1956 Republican Party Convention, Richard Nixon Speech). This statement by Nixon was more in line with the overall strong sentiments of the leaders of the Republican Party. It was clear that there was a lack of a moral, political, or social will on the part of the Southern states to comply with the Supreme Court decision on segregation. In a stroke of cruelty and absurdity from the Southern Republicans, they stated that they would accept language in the 1956 Republican Party Platform stating the 1954 Brown vs. Board of Education decision was the law of the land. They only objected to any written part of the Platform that promised that the Supreme Court decision would be enforced (Anderson, 1964, p. 121).

The Eisenhower administration and the National Republican Party were very concerned about race relations in the United States. In a presidential cabinet meeting on March 9, 1956, the Director of the US Federal Bureau of Investigation, J. E. Hoover, commented on racial tensions and violence in the United States. Hoover suggested that they look on the bright side that there has been a steady decrease in lynching and an expansion of integrated education (US White House, March 9, 1956, p. 2). It was in this meeting that US Attorney General, Herbert Brownell, pointed out it was in Ike's 1956 State of the Union Address when it was stated that a civil rights program would be introduced to Congress by the administration. Here Brownell offered several recommendations that outlined the 1957 CRA: " (1) changes in the voting law so as to extend its coverage to primary elections and allow the Department of Justice to take action under civil law instead of only criminal law; (2) broadening of the general civil rights law to give the Department of Justice a greater choice of approaches to the problem; and (3) establishment of a Civil Rights Division in the Department of Justice to be headed by an Assistant Attorney General" (US White House, March 9, 1956, p. 2).

After a careful review of the proposed civil rights legislation, Ike commented at a April 17, 1956 Legislative meeting that he failed to "imagine anything more moderate or less provocative." Attorney General Brownell had in fact pushed for tougher, more comprehensive legislation. On the other hand, Ike said the civil rights extremists don't understand that troops can be sent but troops cannot operate schools - foreshadowing the dispatch of the Army's 101st Airborne to Little Rock Arkansas Central High School in September of 1957.

Ike sidestepped the opportunity to offer his full-throated support of Brown vs. Board of Education at a news conference in early September of 1956 that asked if he supported the judicial decisions on segregation or only accepted them. "I think it makes no difference whether or not I endorse it. The Constitution is as the Supreme Court interprets it, and I must conform to that and do my best to see that it is carried out in this Country" (Anderson, 1964, p. 131). Much has been made of Ike failing to provide his public, wholehearted support for the Brown vs. Board of Education decision by the US Supreme Court - one of the most momentous decisions the Court has made. However, Ike supported the decision, as he wrote in his memoirs *Waging Peace*, "In this case (referring to Brown vs. Board of Education), I definitely agreed with the unanimous decision" (Eisenhower, 1965, p. 150).

To the credit of Adlai Stevenson, the 1952 and the 1956 Democratic Party nominee for US president, he did state at a speech in Little Rock, AR in 1956 that he fully supported desegregation. This declaration by Stevenson cost him tens of thousands of votes in the South. And it is worth noting that of the 17 states that practiced segregation in the South in 1956, Stevenson won only 7, and in half of those states that Stevenson won the vote was close between him and Ike. Ike appeared to hedge on civil rights for social reasons, personal reasons, and political reasons. (The American Presidency Project, n.d.). Ike comments caustically about Democrats and their approach to civil rights, Democrats "believe, apparently, that the cause of civil rights can be advanced by a formula of much oratory and little performance. We have talked less, but we have acted with patience, human understanding, and with concern for the equal standing of all before the law" (Anderson, 1964, p. 133).

In a response to a request from the American Civil Liberties Union (ACLU) for a campaign statement on civil rights for the 1956 presidential campaign, the ACLU published the following from Ike's campaign with the four points of the latter in the 1957 CRA: "...Creation of a Civil Rights Commission; establishment of a Civil Rights Division in the Justice Department; provision of federal authority to seek injunctive protection of voting rights; and authority for the Justice Department to seek preventive relief in civil rights enforcement" (US Senate Hearings on Civil Rights, 1957, p. 174). Ike is quoted as stating, "...and I will continue to work for it until the full and free exercise of rights and privileges for every United States citizen becomes real and meaningful" (Riley, 1999, p. 187)).

In a Legislative Meeting on the 12th of March in 1957, Republican Senator William Knowland of California (who had been the US senate majority leader from August 1953 to January 1955) told Ike that if the civil rights legislation was to be successful, they had better get it moving soon. And at the Legislative Meeting of June 4, 1957, Republican Representative Kenneth Keating from New York's 38th District noted that some Republicans would oppose the bill altogether, and some would oppose the jury trial amendment. Ike said that it was a mystery to him why any Republicans would oppose such mild proposals. At a Legislative Meeting on the 20th of August in 1957, it was reported that the Republicans in the US House of Representatives would continue to push for a strong bill without accepting a compromise bill.

Ike was a *gradualist* on the monumental American issue of civil rights. Gradualism, of course, was an affront to the African Americans who were lynched, and/or beaten, murdered, denied employment, or any other of a swarm of injustices that were often daily events in the South. Only an enfranchised Anglo-American male would be obdurate enough to refer to themselves as a gradualist when it came to civil rights. Undoubtedly, if you were an African American in the South, you would prefer no hanging at all to a gradual hanging.

However, Ike did not mean that African Americans should be gradually, given their already guaranteed Constitutional rights. Although Ike said a minimal amount in direct public support of Brown (Simon, 2018). Ike did believe that the US Federal Government would enforce the US Supreme Court decision. When Ike referred to the extremists in the civil rights conflict, he meant those individuals who committed acts of violence in the name of segregation or civil rights. Ike pointed out that the Brown vs. Board of Education ruling, which was a galvanizing force of the civil rights movement in the 1950s (both for opponents and proponents), stated that progress on integration would be incremental.

Ike went on, "So, let us remember that there are people who are ready to approach this thing with moderation but with determination to make progress that the Supreme Court asked for. If there ever was a time when we must be patient without being complacent, when we must be understanding of other people's deep emotions as well as our own, this is it. Extremists on either side are not going to help this situation, and we can only believe that the good sense, the common sense of Americans will bring this thing along. The length of time I am not even going to talk about; I don't know anything about the length of time it will take" (The American

Presidency Project, n.d. Public Papers of the US Presidents, p. 303).

Ike was equivocating. Ike stated on numerous occasions that he had lived in the South and that he had respect for their traditions. This seems to say that Ike had respect for segregation as part of the Southern way of life, or that white schoolgirls should not have to sit alongside negro boys in a classroom. "I expect that we are going to make progress, and the Supreme Court itself said it does not expect revolutionary action, suddenly executed. We will make progress, and I am not going to attempt to tell them how it is going to be done" (Eisenhower, Galambos, and Van Ee, 2001, pp. 269-270). Ike communicated about the defiance of the states in complying with the US Supreme Court mandated desegregation, "They were acting in compliance with the law as interpreted by the Supreme Court of the United States under the decision of 1896 (Plessy vs. Ferguson). Now, that has been completely reversed, it is going to take time for them to adjust their thinking and their progress to that" (Eisenhower, Galambos, and Van Ee, 2001, pp. 303-304).

Ike was a cagey politician, and he was a master at dissembling with the press. Ike often portrayed himself as just a regular guy who didn't know much, "Well, I'm not a lawyer," etc. Ike was often asked about segregation, and whether the Republican Party would have to decide between desegregation and segregation. Ike's less than genuine response was that he had sworn to uphold the Constitution. This was an obtuse way of stating that the Supreme Court decision would be upheld. Further, asked if the Eisenhower administration would accelerate desegregation, Ike was bland and evasive when he stated if progress fell short on that issue, he thought the courts would act.

Ike was the moderate obfuscator when he was asked by a reporter if his support for the 1957 CRA would hurt the Republican Party's chances of winning more seats in the South, "...the civil rights bill is a very moderate thing, done in all decency and a simple attempt to study the matter, see where the federal responsibilities lie, and to move in strict accordance with the Supreme Court's decision, and no faster and no further" (Nichols, 2007, p. 201). Ann Whitman, Ike's personal secretary, recalls Ike stating that he, "was not at all unsympathetic to the position that people like Senator Russell take." But she added that Ike was "adamant that the right to vote must be protected" (Caro, 2002, p. 926).

However, Ike fundamentally failed to lead publicly on civil rights or the 1957 CRA, and there was a great deal of anger and lost hope on the part of African American leaders. By June of 1957, Philip Randolph and Martin Luther King had been asking to meet with the president for over a year. Ike failed to respond. Frederic Morrow, Ike's Administrative Officer for Special Projects, and the first African American to hold an executive position at the White House, wrote to Ike's Chief of Staff, Sherman Adams on June 4, 1957, "I can state categorically that the rank and file of negroes in the country feel that the President has deserted them...I feel time is ripe for the President to see two or three outstanding negro leaders, and to let them get off their chests the things that seem to be giving them great concern...Their present feeling is that their acknowledged leadership is being ignored, snubbed, and belittled by the President and his staff" (Caro, 2002, p. 903). Still, Ike was silent. The conventional political wisdom on Capitol Hill was that the 1957 civil rights bill would soon have the same fate as the 1956 civil rights bill. Brownell began drafting civil rights legislation in 1955, and it would be 1957 before it became law. One of the motivators for Brownell was at the federal level, Brownell was unable to act in the Emmett Till murder case. Emmett Till was a 14-

year-old African American boy who was lynched in Mississippi in 1955, after being accused of offending a white woman in her family's grocery store. The vicious brutality of his murder and the fact that his killers were acquitted drew attention to the long history of violent persecution of African Americans in the United States. Brownell knew that the federal justice system had to take a role of authority in a case like this where the local and state courts in the South were so corrupt that they would acquit killers in such a heinous crime (Hitchcock, 2018).

There was a substantial amount of unrest and disagreement within Ike's Cabinet on the contents of the 1957 CRA (Thompson, 1984). Most of his Cabinet members urged moderation, stating that the bill was too aggressive and would fail in the Senate. Attorney General Brownell and the US Justice Department pushed for a much stronger bill - one that gave considerable enforcement power to the US Justice Department. Brownell's civil rights proposal was opposed by Ike's Agricultural Secretary, Ezra Benson. Benson was a strong right-wing conservative leader from Utah who was a member of the Mormon Church. Benson would later become the president of the LDS Church. Benson was a vocal anti-communist and member of the John Birch Society and repeatedly claimed that the communists were using the negroes to foment dissent. In 1968, the segregationist George Wallace, running for US president as a states' rights candidate, asked Benson to be his running mate. (Hitchcock, 2018). Other members of Ike's cabinet supported civil rights, including Fred Seaton, Secretary of the Interior, and James Mitchell, Secretary of Labor.

Brownell was up against some administration officials who were clearly hostile to anti-segregationist legislation. Marion Folsom, the HEW Secretary from Georgia, also opposed the legislation, expressing that the proposed legislation moved too fast. Even John Foster Dulles, US Secretary of State, and probably the most powerful person in Ike's Cabinet, claimed that the Brownell proposal deviated too far from accepted mores. Ike backed Brownell, but he also understood that the segregationist voices in his administration, the Republican Party, and the nation were very powerful. The political and cowardly view among many Republican Party leaders was that any legislation that increased the power of the federal government to prosecute civil rights violations at a state level would increase the anger of Southern whites and cost the Republican Party votes in the next election. Ike was led on the issue of civil rights by the dedication of Brownell, as well as his own personal convictions. But Ike refused to join the movement led by Dr. King and other civil rights leaders.

Ike did not embrace social movements. Ike was a social conservative, and an adherent to a system of social hierarchy, of which he was a privileged member. Yet, as reluctant as he was, Ike ultimately did help the nation forward on civil rights. And it is a great irony that LBJ initially was such a great opponent of the 1957 CRA - weakening the strength of the bill - who would later become known in history as the US president whose greatest good was passing the strongest US civil rights bill in history, the CRA of 1964. LBJ knew he could realize his dream of winning the US presidency by supporting civil rights.

Ike faltered on how aggressive the bill should be - for a couple of reasons - based on the prospect of the bill passing the US Senate (surviving a filibuster) and for fear of inciting violence on the part of segregationists in the South. Brownell and Ike were at odds at times, with Brownell being chastised in at least one instance for speaking out of turn on the exact nature of the bill that the White House (Ike) supported. Yet Eisenhower placed a great deal of trust in Brownell and Brownell's civil rights views. Nonetheless, Brownell was very disappointed that the 1957 CRA was weakened by the Senate.

Ike wanted to nominate Brownell to the US Supreme Court when vacancies arose in 1957 and 1958 but Ike refrained from doing so because Ike believed that the Southern segregationist senators would fight and prevent the nomination. There was a credible threat from a violent segregationist, and the FBI had to provide around-the-clock protection to Brownell and his family. On April 12, 1956, the Richmond Times-Dispatch editorial board published the following: "It is not surprising, that numerous politicians from the North and West, including President Eisenhower and Attorney General Brownell, should be whooping it up for civil rights in this election year. Such gestures have come to be almost as inevitable as the party conventions." Putting aside the contempt that the editors of the Richmond Times-Dispatch had for civil rights, the editors do have a point since the Republican Party did talk a big line about a new civil rights bill but were unable to find the political will to pass legislation since the 1952 convention.

It did seem that the Eisenhower administration was more concerned with its own reelection than the issue of civil rights. The administration was scared that the Southern senators would defeat the bill in the US Senate. However, many liberal Democrats and liberal Republicans in the US Congress blamed the lack of a civil rights bill by 1956 on lack of commitment and leadership in the White House - namely Ike. The US House of Representatives had passed a civil rights bill eight times since 1937. However, all the civil rights bills from the House, up to 1957, were killed upon arrival in the US Senate by the Democratic Party's Southern segregationist senators.

As the Democratic Party candidate for the US presidential elections of 1952 and 1956, Adlai Stevenson had to walk a tightrope on segregation. He needed the Northern liberal wing of the Democratic Party (which supported desegregation) to vote for him and he needed the Southern conservative wing of the Democratic Party (segregationists) to vote for him as well. In a presage to the comments that Lyndon Johnson would later make in 1964 about the US South being lost to the Democratic Party because of LBJ's support for the 1964 CRA, Stevenson said that it would be an 'unmitigated disaster' if the Southern states should leave the Democratic Party because of civil rights conflicts. (Anderson, 1964).

Figure 14: Eisenhower Listening in 1957 CRA Debate.

Ike writes in his memoirs that several Southern senators privately confided to him that they generally supported the 1957 civil rights bill and greater enfranchisement of the African American right to vote. But these same senators also told him that officially and publicly, "I must be, in my state, against every kind of proposal on civil rights of whatever nature" (Eisenhower, 1965, p. 157). Senator Russell of

Georgia publicly stated that he was "prepared to expend the greatest effort ever made in history to prevent passage of this bill in its present form" (Eisenhower, 1965, p. 157).

In a letter dated July 23, 1957 to James F. Byrnes, the segregationist governor of South Carolina, Ike equivocally states that the 1957 CRA is to provide a moderate approach to a difficult problem and to make haste slowly in seeking to meet it. Ike kicks the can again in the letter to Governor Byrnes by stating that the jury trial issue in the 1957 CRA is essentially a legal matter (Eisenhower, 1957).

The immediate backdrop for the 1957 CRA was Brown vs. Board of Education, in which the US Supreme Court struck down the longstanding separate but equal position as unconstitutional and thus made segregation of schools illegal. The US Southern states were furious with the ruling and were non-compliant. Segregation was established by the US Confederate states after the US Civil War as a means of maintaining white supremacy in all aspects of life. A fundamental aspect of the Brown vs. Board of Education ruling by the US Supreme Court is that it criminalized discrimination in the form of segregation in the South. This meant that the inhuman social system in the South had become outlawed. To many whites in the South, this was an all-out assault by the US Federal Government on their way of life.

The Brown vs. Board of Education US Supreme Court ruling is closely connected to the US Supreme Court Ruling of Plessy vs. Ferguson. *Plessy vs. Ferguson*, 163 US 537 (1896), was a major ruling by the Supreme Court that upheld the constitutionality of racial segregation laws for public facilities if the segregated facilities were equal in quality. This ruling was the doctrine known as *separate but equal*. The Court's decision legitimized the many state laws establishing racial segregation passed in the American South after the Civil War Reconstruction Era (1865–1877). The Southern segregationist states used Plessy vs. Ferguson to defend segregation and referred to the ruling as the law of the land. This argument had some merit, inasmuch as Plessy vs. Ferguson was the law of the land.

In a personal letter that Ike wrote to his long-time friend, Swede Hazlet, Ike tells a story illustrating his view on separate but equal and Brown vs. Board of Education. "For example, a violent exponent of the segregation doctrine was in my office one day. During his visit, he delivered an impassioned talk about the sanctity of the 1896 decision by the US Supreme Court. At a pause in his oration, I merely asked, 'Then why is the 1954 decision not equally sacrosanct?' He stuttered and said, 'There were then wise men on the Court. Now we have politicians.' I replied, 'Can you name one man on the 1896 Court who made the decision?' He just looked at me in consternation and the subject was dropped" (Eisenhower, 1957, p. 323).

In that same letter, Ike wrote on July 22, 1957, "I think no other single event has so disturbed the domestic scene in many years as did the Supreme Court decision of 1954 in the school segregation case. That decision and similar ones have interpreted the Constitution in such a fashion as to put heavier responsibilities than before on the Federal Government in the matter of assuring to each citizen his guaranteed Constitutional rights." Ike goes on to write to Swede:

> My approach to the many problems has been dictated by several obvious truths.
> (a) Laws are rarely effective unless they represent the will of the majority. (b) When emotions are deeply stirred, logic, and reason

must operate gradually. (c) School segregation itself was, according to the Supreme Court of 1896 (Separate but Equal), completely Constitutional until the reversal of that decision was accomplished in 1954. The decision of 1896 gave a cloak of legality to segregation in all its forms. (d) After threescore years of living under these patterns, it is impossible to expect complete and instant reversal of conduct by mere decision of the Supreme Court. (Eisenhower, 1957, p. 186). (Abbreviated by the author for emphasis.)

All this background on the racial divisions in the South in the context of Brown vs. Board of Education is important because it was in this social upheaval that Ike was determined to pass a civil rights act in the US Congress. United States segregation was a system of subjugation of African Americans by white Americans in the South. The Constitutional right of African Americans to vote was damned under the system of Southern segregation.

The 1957 CRA was signed by President Eisenhower on September 9, 1957. Integration of the Little Rock, Arkansas Central High School began on September 4, 1957. On the order of the segregationist, Governor Orvil Faubus, the Arkansas National Guard prevented black students from entering the school. On September 24, 1957, Eisenhower sent the 101st Airborne Division of the US Army to protect the students. Eisenhower nationalized the 10,000 members of the Arkansas National Guard, thereby taking control of the Guard away from Governor Faubus (Caro, 2002).

The Southern states had a complicated relationship with the US Federal Government. When it came to school reform and desegregation the federal government was a tyrannical authority ready to put jackboots on the ground to deny Southerners their God-granted right to practice racial discrimination. However, when it came to the largesse of the federal government to the state governments of the US South - money to build roads, hospitals, schools, airports, and government defense contracts – United States federal intervention in the form of money was welcomed.

Southern senators renewed their vows to block all civil rights legislation, a vow they vocalized in the 1956 March Manifesto, also known as the Southern Manifesto. The Southern Manifesto opposed racial integration in public places. It was signed by 101 congressmen (99 Southern Democrats and 2 Republicans). The Southern Manifesto accused the US Supreme Court of a clear abuse of judicial power in its 1954 Brown vs. Board of Education ruling. And the signers of the Southern Manifesto pledged that they would do everything in their power to reverse the US Supreme Court decision.

In a stunning display of lies, the Southern Manifesto stated, "This unwarranted exercise of power by the Court, contrary to the Constitution, is creating chaos and confusion in the States principally affected. It is destroying the amicable relations between the white and Negro races created through 90 years of patient effort by the good people of both races. It has planted hatred and suspicion where there has been heretofore friendship and understanding" (Hitchcock, 2018, p. 241). Brownell later noted in his memoirs that Section 3 of the 1957 CRA "gave the US Attorney General direct authority to enforce Court orders to desegregate public schools and to enter cases such as the Emmett Till murder." Brownell said he admired Ike because Ike supported sending the 1957 bill to Congress even though his presidential cabinet was split on the issue (Hitchcock, 2018, p. 241).

According to the Memorandum for the President dated August 6, 1957, at the present stage of its consideration by the Senate, the civil rights bill (H.R 6127) contained five provisions:

> I. A provision containing a bipartisan Commission on Civil Rights... with power (a) to investigate allegations of denial of the right to vote...The Commission is given the power to issue subpoenas and administer oaths to witnesses...
>
> II. A provision authorizing the appointment of an additional Assistant Attorney General to perform such functions as the Attorney General may direct...
>
> III. A provision making unlawful threats, intimidation, or coercion for the purpose of interfering with the right to vote in Federal elections...
>
> IV. A provision purporting to give negroes a right which they already have - the right to serve on Federal juries...
>
> V. A provision requiring that all trials for criminal contempt in injunction suits brought by the United States, upon demand of the person charged with such contempt, be before a jury... (The White House August 6, 1957).

Figure 15: The Little Rock Nine Escorted to School in Arkansas by the US National Guard.

The final version of the 1957 CRA that Ike signed into law on September 9, 1957 is as follows: (1) Created, with a two-year life, the six-member Civil Rights Commission; (2) set up a Civil Rights Division in the Justice Department; (3) extended the jurisdiction of the district courts to include and civil action begun to secure relief under any act of Congress providing for the protection of civil rights, including the right to vote; (4) empowered the US Attorney General to seek an injunction when an individual had been deprived of the right to vote; and (5) included the jury trial compromise to which the Republican and Democratic leaders had agreed.

Two short weeks later, Ike sent the US Army 101st Airborne Division to Little Rock, Arkansas to enforce United States school desegregation. Although this action was some time in coming, and it had nothing to do with the 1957 CRA. It was now made clear that Ike would use the full force of the US Federal Government to enforce civil rights in the South.

The segregationists decided on a couple of strategies to oppose civil rights legislation. The segregationists sought to garner overall public support to prevent the legislation by arguing that the 1957 CRA would empower the US president (Ike) to use the force of US troops against its own citizens in the South by forcing desegregation on the people of the South. The other tactic was to claim that the 1957 CRA would deny the Southern people the constitutional right of trial by jury. The segregationists insisted that a trial by jury was uncompromisable. The disingenuous nature of this demand under the circumstances was clear because, in the Deep South, African Americans were prevented from sitting on juries. Therefore, any trial of a white person made up of a jury of white persons in the Deep South alleging that the white defendant had denied an African American his or her voting rights, would invariably end with a verdict of 'not guilty.' Senator Harry Byrd of Virginia referred to Ike's plan for civil rights legislation as: "...a travesty of justice to attempt the protection of civil rights for any one group through a process which denies a liberty equally precious-that of a trial by jury" (Nichols, 2007, p. 150). The Eisenhower administration was cornered into responding to these allegations by stating "...if a state discharges its obligations under the 14th and 15th Amendments, there will be no room for federal intervention" (Nichols, 2008, p. 155).

On the floor of the US Senate, US Senator Richard Russell from Georgia (The New York Times referred to Senator Russell as the "Leader of a Lost Cause") accused Attorney General Brownell of creating a deceptive piece of legislation that was cunningly designed to destroy the system of separation of the races in the Southern states at the point of a bayonet (Nichols, 2008, p. 155). LBJ was the arbiter of the 1957 CRA in the US Congress. The votes for the bill, in all its versions, existed in the US House of Representatives.

Indeed, the House passed several versions of it in 1956 and 1957. The fight would be in the US Senate. LBJ, a powerful Texas Democratic senator, was supportive of segregation and his fellow segregationists. He had to accept the bill from the Eisenhower administration and "take out its teeth." Then

LBJ had to convince his fellow segregationists to allow the toothless civil rights bill to come to the Senate floor for a vote. His fellow segregationists could refrain from voting for the bill, but they did need to let it pass, as there were enough Northern Democrats and moderate Republicans to pass it. In the wake of his success, Johnson would have greater prominence in the South and the North, and then ride this success to the White House as president (Hitchcock 2018).

Figure 16: LBJ and Senator Richard Russel

The relentless attack by US senators on the 1957 CRA went beyond the senators from the former Confederacy. At one point, one of the most conservative Republican senators in the US Senate, Senator Bourke Hickenlooper from Iowa stood up and told his colleagues that the passage of the Brownell Bill would be "a violation of the civil rights of the white race." While his colleague, Democratic Olin Johnson, senator (and former governor) of South Carolina, asked his fellow senators, "Senators, do you want to be responsible for a second Reconstruction?" (Caro, 2002, p. 918). The segregationist senators and other Southern leaders had some success in characterizing Part 3 of the bill as a section that would mandate the unwarranted expansion of federal power.

Part Three of the CRA, which was the Provision of federal authority to seek injunctive protection of voting rights was opposed by several Republican legislative leaders because they viewed it as an invitation for the federal government to use troops to enforce voting rights. The president told leaders "the intent is simply that the orders of the federal courts would be supported." Ike went on later to further describe Part Three as "a reasonable program of assistance in efforts to protect other constitutional rights of our citizens" (Nichols, 2011, p.158).

In a Memorandum for the President dated August 15, 1957 the US Justice Department details the Compromise Civil Rights Proposal: (1) Reinstate Part III, which would permit the US Attorney General to seek injunctions in civil rights cases other than voting cases where the local authorities request the Attorney General to do so. (2) In criminal contempt cases, it would provide that where the penalty imposed is imprisonment for not in excess of 90 days or a fine in excess of $300, and the trial for contempt would be without a jury. In criminal contempt cases, there would be a trial by jury (Morgan, 1957, p. 1).

Val Washington, the Republican National Committee's minority programs director, wrote that he was "troubled by the compromise talk on the civil rights bill." And in personal communication to Ike, Val Washington was acerbic and accurate in telling Ike, "Let me say that your civil rights bill is a very moderate one, so what is there to compromise?" (Caro, 2002, p. 927). LBJ then told Ike that he had the votes to kill the bill if Part Three remained in the legislation. Ike heeded LBJ's threat and agreed to drop the provision. The Senate then voted 52-38 to remove part three from the bill. Brownell was unhappy with the compromise and with some contempt referred to Ike's decision to do so as a political decision (Nichols, 2011).

Ike understood that he had to make difficult decisions on the fate of the 1957 civil rights bill and the fate of his overall legislative agenda. LBJ made it clear to the president that if Ike refused to water down Section Three of the bill, LBJ would block other administration legislative priorities. Regarding Section Three of the bill, Ike responded to a reporter's question that asked if Section Three was the most important part of the bill because it would empower the federal government to enforce school desegregation: "Well, no...I personally believe if you try to go too far too fast in laws in this delicate field that has involved the emotions of so many million Americans, you are making a mistake."

At the same time, behind the scenes, Vice President Richard Nixon was working with the Republican senators to prevent writing a jury trial amendment into Section Four of the bill. Senator Knowland and VP Nixon worked together to prevent several Republican senators from voting in favor of the amendment. Nixon understood the stakes with the jury trial amendment and was maneuvering with Knowland and several leading Democratic senators to stand firm to avoid a compromise on the jury trial amendment (Caro, 2002).

The Southern senators refused to compromise. Senator Richard Russell and his Southern colleagues would accept nothing less than a guarantee of a jury trial. LBJ was undeterred. LBJ reached out to numerous legal minds to find a way out of the impasse. Ben Cohen, one of the key legal minds of New Deal legislation, contacted LBJ and relayed to LBJ a legal article he had read by a University of Wisconsin Law Professor, Carl A. Auerbach. Auerbach wrote that jury trials are only required in criminal contempt proceedings. Jury trials are nonessential in civil contempt proceedings. Yet, civil contempt proceedings could also be used to enforce civil rights. Thus, if a provision for civil contempt could be written into the bill, the stalemate could be broken. Add to this, the bill would also include a restoration of labor union striker's right to a jury trial that had been taken away with the Taft-Hartley Act, and LBJ had even greater ground to get more votes for the 1957 CRA (Caro, 2002).

At one point, Wayne Morse, the liberal senator from Oregon, sought to block a unanimous consent agreement on a bill that some Southerners wanted. LBJ told Morse: "Look, you're going to be in the position of wanting (their) support in the future. This (the jury trial amendment) isn't that hurtful to your state's interest or your own convictions. Don't build it up into a blockage" (Caro, 2002, p. 956). LBJ went on to tell more of his liberal Democratic colleagues, "Give them the vote, that's what matters. Then things will change, you'll see." LBJ worked to convince his colleagues in the Senate Chamber that the Southern senators had to have the jury trial amendment, or the bill was dead.

LBJ had some whiplash because as he was telling his Southern colleagues that their filibuster of the civil rights bill would fail, he was telling other colleagues that they lacked the votes to beat a filibuster. LBJ told his liberal colleagues that if they passed this weaker civil rights bill, stronger civil rights bills would follow. LBJ in turn told his segregationist friends that if they failed to support this weaker bill that a stronger, less desirable one (to them) would surely follow. LBJ was correct because there were stronger civil rights bills that followed in 1960, 1964, 1965, 1968, and 1991. Three years later, the Civil Rights Act of 1960 expanded the enforcement powers of the Civil Rights Act of 1957 and introduced criminal penalties for obstructing federal court orders. It also extended the Civil Rights Commission for two years and required voting and registration records for federal elections be preserved.

The segregationist senators, buoyed by this compromise on Section III of the CRA, doubled down on their effort to get a jury trial provision into part four of the bill. This was too far for Ike and the Republican Party leaders, and they stated that they should reject "any attempt to incorporate a jury trial amendment in the right to vote section of the bill and thus nullify the purpose of the legislation." It was clear to all involved that a provision to the bill requiring a jury trial would successfully enable the South to continue to deny the right to vote to African Americans and effectively make meaningless the entire 1957 CRA. In a show of his refusal to nullify the CRA Ike stated: "I believe that the United States must make certain that every citizen who is entitled to vote under the Constitution is actually given that right. I believe also that in sustaining that right, we must sustain the power of the Federal judges in whose hands such cases would fall. So, I do not believe in any amendment to section 4 of the bill" (Nichols, 2008, p. 160).

LBJ was fully behind segregationist Senator Richard Russell of Georgia in his demand for a jury trial in section 4 of the bill. Senate Minority leader Knowland demanded that the senators support President Eisenhower. LBJ cynically responded by stating that the people of America would reject "that a man can be publicly branded as a criminal without a jury trial" (Nichols, 2008, p. 160).

On August 1, 1957, the US Senate voted 51-47 to amend the civil rights bill to require a jury trial for the prosecution of criminal contempt for voting rights violations. VP Nixon referred to this vote as one of the saddest days in the Senate "because it was a vote against the right to vote." It was bewildering that even the most liberal voices in the Senate, Hubert Humphrey of Minnesota and Paul Douglas of Illinois, voted in favor of the amendment, ostensibly because they were afraid of the label of anti-civil liberties by opposing 'due process' in the form of a jury trial. In the August 2, 1957 presidential cabinet meeting, Ike was furious and said, "not much forgiveness in my soul." Ike called the vote bitterly disappointing. Ike hinted that he would veto the bill as it stood. (Eisenhower and Hagerty, August 2, 1957).

Deputy Attorney General William P. Rogers referred to the hollowed-out bill as "a monstrosity-the most irresponsible bill I have seen in Washington." Rogers went on to say that the bill "gave policemen a gun but no bullets" (Eisenhower, 1965, p. 159). In a press release issued by James C. Hagerty, Press Secretary to the president, dated August 2, 1957 President Eisenhower makes a forceful statement of his anger at the failed Senate vote of the CRA: "The result cannot fail to be bitterly disappointing to those many millions of Americans who realized that without the minimum protection that was projected in Section V of the bill as it passed the House of Representatives, many Americans will continue, in effect, to be disenfranchised" (Hitchcock, 2018, p. 358). Val Washington blamed LBJ and wrote to LBJ that the civil rights bill "was emasculated by adroit handling of you with the aid of other Democrat leaders." Washington went on to tell LBJ, "If a Southern jury would not convict confessed kidnappers of Emmet Till after he was found murdered, why would they convict an election official for refusing to give a negro the right of suffrage?" (Nichols, 2008, p. 162).

The famous African American Major League Baseball player Jackie Robinson wrote to tell Ike: "Am opposed to the civil rights bill in its present form. I have been in touch with a number of my friends. We disagree that half a loaf is better than none. Have waited this long for a bill with meaning - we can wait a little longer." And to Ike from A. Philip Randolph, president of the union of the Brotherhood of

Sleeping Car Porters: "In the name of the officials of the Brotherhood of Sleeping Car Porters, urge veto of civil rights bill. It is worse than no bill at all." The Reverend W.H. Jernigan, Chairman, Executive Board of the National Fraternal Council of Churches (representing 10 million African American churchgoers) "Ninety percent of colored Americans favor the bill passed by the House. Personally, I will have no bill passed at this Congress than the one passed by the Senate" (Eisenhower, 1965, p. 101).

At an August 6, 1957, legislative meeting, Ike stated, "We ought to stand firm" on passing the bill enact, minus part three. Congressional leaders told Ike they would get the voting rights provision restored to its original form with the jury trial requirement. Ike considered the problems that would arise if he vetoed the bill. Half of something is better than half of nothing. Although, half of something might virtually be nothing. The bill was presented to the American people as a step forward in civil rights, and Ike could not afford to veto it and be unsupportive of this "step forward."

Liberal Democrats were sheepish about their failure to fight harder for a stronger version of the bill. They tried to shift the blame to Ike by saying that if Ike had shown greater stamina for the bill, that it would still be a strong bill. Hubert Humphrey blamed Ike for the failure: "...if the President gives his full weight and prestige behind the bill." Humphrey went on to excoriate Ike: "...vacillated and oscillated, procrastinated and dawdled. He was hesitant and confused. With this type of leadership, it is no wonder that administration supporters were unable to maintain the initiative in this fight" (Nichols, 2008, p. 163). Humphrey, although he voted against the deletion of part three and opposed the jury trial amendment of the bill, he ultimately voted in favor of the diminished bill claiming that "This bill, even in its present form, is better than no bill at all."

In Good Faith

Disgruntled Republican Congressional leaders met with Ike on August 13, 1957. The idea was floated that the administration withdraw the bill and reintroduce it in 1958. Ike exploded: "Hell of a thing. Here are 18 Southern senators who can bamboozle the entire Senate." Ike saved his greatest ire for LBJ: "When someone tries to hit me over the head with a brickbat, I start looking around for something to hit him with." Ironically, Ike would later thank LBJ for his prowess in passing the 1957 CRA in the Senate. There was an abundance of irony (Nichols, 2008, p. 164).

The Republican leadership decided on a final strategy that would push through with debate in Congress in order to get a stronger bill. The Republicans would foment dissent within the Democrat Party ranks by resubmitting part three of the original bill - increasing the authority of the US Attorney General to prosecute the violation of civil rights, including the failure to desegregate. If the bill was defeated, the Democrats could be blamed. Another deadlock ensued. The US Justice Department intervened to help break the stalemate on August 16, 1957 and proposed to the president that in contempt cases involving civil rights cases, a federal judge could try a defendant without a jury if the punishment avoided a fine of more than $300 or imprisonment of more than 90 days.

LBJ gave the impression that he originated and put forth the compromise proposal. The New York Times praised the negotiation skills of LBJ when it was the administration that broke the logjam. As President Ronald Reagan stated years later, "There is no limit to the amount of good that you can do if you don't care who gets the credit." LBJ was ready to get the bill signed into law and called Ike on August 23, 1957 to tell him that he (Ike) could get 'key people' to agree' to a compromise on the civil rights bill of $300 and 45 days as the threshold for the jury trial in contempt cases. LBJ asked Ike if 'his boys' would agree to the terms. Ike asked for 10 minutes and then called Senator Knowland and Representative Martin and got their consent. Ike called LBJ back and confirmed the deal (Eisenhower, 1957). LBJ thanked Eisenhower for the public and private pressure and for applying the force of the moral imperative of the African American voting franchise.

On August 29, 1957, the US Senate passed the final version of the bill on a vote of 60-15, 37 Republicans and 23 Democrats, Ike's civil rights coalition. 15 Southern senators opposed the bill, including Senator Strom Thurmond of South Carolina, who staged a 24-hour, 18-minute filibuster, still the longest filibuster ever in the US Senate. Senator Thurman collapsed on the Senate floor. African American Congressman Adam Clayton Powell, Jr. of New York wrote that Ike had "kept his word to me 100%" on the 1957 Civil Rights Act. "Martin Luther King, Jr. said, I have come to the conclusion that the present bill is far better than no bill at all" (Hitchcock, 2018, p. 360).

LBJ wanted a moderate CRA in 1957. And, in good part, it was widely known that LBJ wanted the 1957 CRA bill to advance his own chances of winning the White House in 1960. As the Majority Leader of the US Senate, LBJ had tremendous power over whether a bill made it to the floor, was killed, allowed to proceed, or filibustered. But it was complicated because LBJ also believed that the 1957 CRA was the right thing to do. LBJ, like most politicians (and most people), was opportunistic. The US civil rights activist, Roy Wilkins, worked with LBJ on many occasions and famously captured the complicated nature of LBJ by saying, "With Johnson, you never knew if he was out to lift your heart or your wallet" (Nichols, 2008, p. 145).

In Good Faith

Ike had a pretty good sense of Johnson's "personal equation" and used that equation to his advantage in getting the 1957 CRA passed. Ike believed that Johnson had an "extreme readiness to be opportunistic about politics." And Ike was aware that Johnson also understood political consequences. Thus, Johnson was willing to take on the civil rights issue (as best he could) as a cause, understanding the benefits that would accrue and the costs that would be applied to his own political career. We see going forward that Johnson put himself firmly in history as the most successful president in the area of civil rights. Following the passage of the 1957 CRA bill, LBJ showed great patronage to those who supported his strategy and voted with him on the bill. He named allies to desirable committees in the Senate. Senator Frank Church of Idaho said that LBJ was ebullient after the passage of the 1957 CRA: "He (LBJ) would pick you up and wrap his arms around you and just squeeze the air out" (Caro, 2002, p. 988).

With Part Three of the bill removed, the bill really only dealt with voting rights. Civil rights lawyer Joe Rauh, a veteran of numerous civil rights laws in the United States is quoted as stating: "When Johnson took Part III out of the House bill, he set back integration in the South for seven years. Part III passed in 1964 - the Part III that was taken out in 1957 in essence became part of the 1964 Act. But for seven years, there was no federal power to bring injunctive suits" (Caro, 2002, p. 1002).

Robert Caro, the monumental biographer of LBJ writes in his third book about LBJ, *Master of the Senate*, that LBJ "had obtained the political gain that his political ambition demanded." Caro goes on to write that there was another greater significance to the 1957 CRA above and beyond the presidential ambitions of LBJ: "And there was another reason-the most important reason of all-that the Civil Rights

Act of 1957 meant hope. There may have only been meager significance in the Act itself, but there was massive significance in what the fight for the Act's passage had revealed about the potentialities of the man who led that fight, about the possibilities that lay within that man for the advancement of social justice in America" (Caro, 2002, p. 1009).

When Ike signed the 1957 CRA into law on September 9, 1957 it was joyless. Ike signed the bill with little pride in the accomplishment. The US South saw the bill as a win for them, having significantly weakened Parts 3 and 4. Nonetheless, the Citizens' Councils of America (their motto was States Rights and Racial Integrity), which was a widespread white supremacist organization formed after the 1954 Supreme Court decision and found primarily in the South, called the 1957 CRA "coercive and vicious." Senator Richard Russell claimed that his leadership in taking the teeth out of the bill was "the greatest victory of his 25 years in the Senate." The African American newspaper, the Chicago Defender, called the 1957 CRA a Confederate Victory (Hitchcock, 2018, p. 359). The significant weakening of Section 4 of the Act meant that in cases where there were significant violations of the right to vote by white Southerners against African Americans, and a judge sought to punish offenders with real jail time, the defendant could be certain that he would have a jury of his fellow white Southerners to acquit him of any wrongdoing.

In his Principled Strong Negotiation, Eisenhower was able to separate the people from the problem. In other words, Eisenhower avoided condemning the segregationists personally but rather the practice of preventing blacks from voting in the South. Eisenhower was committed to upholding the rule of law. Eisenhower focused on interests and avoided positions. He consistently stated that it was in the interests of all and American democracy for all persons to exercise their constitutional right to vote. Eisenhower based the outcome on objective criteria – full voting rights for all. Ultimately, the position of the segregationists was defending an immoral and defenseless practice, which the segregationists unrelentingly called their "way of life" (King, 1992, p. 264).

Figure 17: June 23, 1958 - Dwight D. Eisenhower receives a group of prominent civil rights leaders. Left to Right: Dr. Martin Luther King, Jr., E. Frederic Morrow, Dwight D. Eisenhower, and A. Philip Randolph.

The Act did afford protections to African Americans and their right to vote. And the Act was the first in several more civil rights acts that followed up until 2006. All the subsequent civil rights acts were much stronger than the 1957 Act, especially the most well-known of all, the 1964 Civil Rights Act. The Civil Rights Act of 1964 is a landmark civil rights and labor law in the United States which outlaws discrimination based on race, color, religion, sex, or national origin. It prohibits unequal application of voter registration requirements, and racial segregation in schools, employment, and public accommodations.

Dr. Martin Luther King, Jr. welcomed what little progress the 1957 CRA brought by writing this about it: "I am sure we will soon emerge from the bleak and desolate midnight of man's inhumanity to man to the bright and glittering daybreak of freedom and justice for all men."

Ike failed to be forceful in getting the 1957 CRA passed earlier. And Ike failed to use enough of his 'principled authority' to push the passage of the CRA much sooner.

Chapter 5
The Steel Strike of 1959: Be an Honest Broker with Your Self Interest

The Steel Strike of 1959 set the United Steelworkers of America (USWA) against major US steelworks companies. The strike lasted 116 days from July to November 1959. The 1959 Steel Strike remains the largest work stoppage in US history, with ~500,000 steelworkers closing all steel mills in the United States. The strike had a widespread and dramatic effect on the United States economy. Ike was determined to see the 1959 Steel Strike end. He directed and negotiated from behind the scenes and in public to accelerate a new contract between USWA and the US steel corporations.

At the heart of the strike was the US steel industry management demand that the Union give up an employment contract clause (2 (b)) which limited management's ability to change the number of workers assigned to a task or to introduce new work rules or machinery which would save labor. To management, the clause prevented improvements in efficiency in the production of steel. To United Steel Workers of America, the removal of the clause meant a step to eliminate steelworker jobs

The 1959 US Steel Strike devastated the United States steel industry. For four months, almost 85% of United States steel production was shut down. Steel-consuming sectors in the United States began to purchase steel from Japan and Korea. The US steel industry failed to fully recover. The USWA may have won what they wanted but lost their long-term livelihoods in the bargain. The two sides fought, and both sides lost as did the US economy. In this story, Eisenhower was an honest broker in these negotiations. He played a major role behind the scenes getting the two sides together, more than was generally made public. Ike succeeded in bringing the sides together and ultimately ending the strike.

Figure 18: Steel Mills in Gary in 1973, Indiana. Photo by Paul Sequeira.

The Steel Strike of 1959 is a story of three powerful entities in the United States - the US Federal Government, the US steel manufacturers, and the steelworker's union which represented the united steelworkers of America. These three powerful forces had conflicting interests in the dispute. President Eisenhower led the US Federal Government. The 12 major US steel companies consisted of ARMCO Steel Company, US Steel Corporation, Bethlehem Steel Corporation, Jones and Laughlin Steel Corporation, Youngstown Sheet and Tube Company, Republic Steel Company, Inland Steel Company, Great Lakes Steel Corporation, Kaiser Steel Corporation, Colorado Fuel and Iron Corporation, Wheeling Steel Corporation, and Allegheny Ludlum Steel Corporation. The president of the USWA was David McDonald.

Through the late 1940s and 1950s, the US steel industry had been operating on 3-year contracts. When the 1956 contract (which increased hourly employment costs by 30% over three years and increased the cost of steel commensurately) (Hall, 1979) came up in 1959, the US economy was weaker than before. The US steel companies were only operating at two-thirds capacity. The steel companies were thus able to hold out for lower wage increases. The 116-day strike kept half a million steelworkers from working. By the end of the strike, another 250,000 workers in steel-dependent industries were laid off. United States steelworkers were paid well - higher than any other manufacturing industry in the United States except for auto workers. The final settlement in 1960, although there was a lower wage increase, did strengthen the steelworkers' pension benefits and health care benefits. Job security and lifetime benefits became more of a focus for the union than wage increases.

Some of the most influential men in US history made their riches in the steel industry, including Andrew Carnegie. Carnegie established the Carnegie Steel Company which became the US Steel Corporation when J.P. Morgan bought it (along with the Federal Steel Company and the National Steel Company), then the largest United States steel maker. The US Steel Corporation (USS) became the largest corporation in the world. USS remains the second-largest United States steel producer behind Nucor Steel. In 1959, for the first time, the United States imported more steel than it exported. Since the US Steel Strike of 1959, the United States has been a net importer of steel.

The zenith of the United States steel industry was 1945 when the United States produced almost two-thirds of the steel in the world. By 1959, that number had dropped to about 25%. In 2020, the United States produced only five percent of the world's steel. The United States steel industry's employment peaked in 1953 with about 650,000 workers. In 2020 that number was about 83,000 workers or about 12% of the number of workers it once was. In 1959, the US steel industry was the single largest manufacturing sector in the United States. Many elements contributed to the overall decline of the US steel industry. The 1959 Steel Strike tragically illustrates several elements and the profound impact on the US national economy. The industry employed hundreds of thousands, creating great cities like Pittsburgh, Youngstown, and Gary, IN (named after lawyer Elbert Henry Gary who founded the United States Steel Corporation) (Tiffany, 1988).

Steel markets are immense, complex, and largely staid - its demand as a product in an industrialized economy rises and falls depending on larger economic conditions. It is a "producer's good subject to cyclic demand." Steel pricing is *inelastic* because a decline in its price to buyers does not increase demand. Therefore, historically steel producers have long sought consistent price stability in the industry. There are tremendous, fixed costs of production in steelmaking. Producers have the mills running at full capacity to decrease the incremental costs of production and increase profits. One of the greatest variable costs of input into the production of steel is labor. Like many industries in the United States that became organized in the late 1800s and early 1900s, there was a long and violent fight by steelworkers to improve their working conditions.

The Homestead Strike of 1892 showed the determination of steel magnate Andrew Carnegie to maintain long hours and low pay for steelworkers. The Carnegie Steel Corporation had recently made concessions to the workers in pay and work hours. But Andrew Carnegie was determined to reverse those concessions, and in 1892 increased production demands on the workers. The workers refused to comply.

There were violent clashes between steelworkers and the Pinkerton security forces hired by Carnegie. Eventually, Carnegie appealed to Ohio Governor William Stone, who sent eight thousand men from the state militia to break the strike. There were more strikes, including a bitter strike in 1919 which shut down half of the steel production in the United States. Eventually, the steel producers broke the strike, subjugating the steelworkers for another 15 years. Until 1923, steelworkers were working in dangerous conditions seven days per week, 12 hours per day. It was another 20 years before a strong, national union of steelworkers could compel better working conditions and better pay.

The United Steel Workers of America was founded on May 22, 1942, in Cleveland, OH. It took almost ten years of struggle for the USW to successfully earn the right to collectively bargain with all the steel makers, which ultimately earned the USW members higher wages and paid vacations. These gains were hard-fought and even today the median wage of a USWA member is 53k/year, which is well above the United States average income of 31k. USWA members earned 70% more than the average United States worker in 2020.

The United States steel industry grew dramatically during WWII and in the postwar years. The Franklin Delano Roosevelt (FDR) administration contributed greatly to the expansion of the US steel industry. In 1941, the US government gave 1.1 billion dollars to expand the US steel industry to add 15.2 million tons of steel-making capacity for the war effort. The United States government financed and built new steel mills. At the end of WWII, the mills were sold to private steel corporations at a considerable loss to the US governement. The single largest private entity financial beneficiary of this arrangement was the US Steel Corporation (Tiffany, 1988).

There was a great deal of inflation following WWII for most consumer goods and services. But because of federal price controls on steel, steel products had less inflation than other consumer goods. The price controls on the steel industry allowed for relative industry stability during and immediately following WWII. However, with the 1948 election of Harry S. Truman as the 33rd president of the United States, the steel industry executives feared that Truman would show too much deference to the labor unions. The steel industry executives feared that a Truman administration would bring price controls, controlled allocation of steel to certain customers, governmental control of mills, price controls to combat inflation, more taxes on the profits, anti-trust suits, and pro-labor legislation. Indeed, these concerns were warranted as Truman did seek to nationalize the steel mills.

A nationwide strike by the USWA was planned for April 9, 1952. Just before the strike, President Truman, by executive order, nationalized the entire United States steel industry. The steel companies immediately sued, and in a major decision, the US Supreme Court ruled on June 2, 1952 that President Truman lacked the executive authority to seize the steel mills. The strike and attempted nationalization ended where it had begun with the USWA gaining some modest wage and benefit increases. But there were tremendous economic consequences for the nation. Around 1.5 million people lost their jobs before steel production resumed. The estimated economic loss was about 4 billion dollars. But the USWA considered it a win. Truman protected the union, the Taft Hartley Act was not invoked, and the USWA now had union shops (Tiffany, 1988). The public perception of the United States steel industry was very good in the 1950s. The general public considered the US steel industry the most essential production sector in the United States economy (Tiffany, 1988).

The Eisenhower administration supported the US steel industry, but Ike opposed trade barriers. This hurt the US steel industry, as imports of steel continued being less expensive than US manufacturing. Ike was a strong believer in the ability of free trade to help prevent international conflict and help prevent the spread of international communism. "Trade not aid" was the Eisenhower administration slogan. Yet, in many cases, the US trade organizations were helping other nations like Japan establish manufacturing capacity and trade to the United States, which undercut the prices of US steel manufacturers at home. US steelmakers fought to maintain higher prices for their goods and the major steel buyers such as the auto, construction, and heavy equipment industries naturally bought the less expensive product, which was imported steel (Tiffany, 1988).

Inflation in the steel industry and the United States economy, in general, was growing in the 1950s. There was a wage-price spiral in the US steel industry. And the US Congress began having many hearings on the subject as there were more price hikes of steel in the 1950s. When the US steel industry conceded a wage increase to US steelworkers the increased cost of production was passed on to the consumers. The failure to innovate and reduce labor costs were major contributors to the US steel industry decline in the 1950s. Management saw the USWA as the cause of the wage-price spiral in steel. The USWA believed that the only thing that management wanted was to break the union. Ike wanted economic vitality for the nation (Tiffany, 1988).

Lou Villaire

The Labor-Management Relations Act of 1947, better known as the Taft–Hartley Act, is a United States federal law that restricts the activities and power of labor unions. It was enacted by the 80th United States Congress over the veto of President Harry S. Truman, becoming law on June 23, 1947. The Act has long been controversial because the law is rightfully seen by labor unions as a law that reduces their power. Taft-Hartley was introduced in the US Congress in the aftermath of a major strike wave in 1945 and 1946 in the United States. Though it was enacted by the Republican-controlled 80th Congress, the law received significant support from congressional Democrats, many of whom joined with their Republican colleagues in voting to override Truman's veto of the Taft-Hartley. The act continued to generate opposition after Truman left office, but it remains in effect today. The Taft-Hartley Act reserved the rights of labor unions to organize and bargain collectively but outlawed closed shops, giving workers the right to decline to join a union. The Act also authorizes the president to intervene in strikes or potential strikes that create a national emergency.

It was on September 28, 1959, that Eisenhower met privately with McDonald and Arthur Goldberg and threatened to invoke the back-to-work provisions of the Taft-Hartley Act. McDonald was unwilling to budge on Section 2(b) without concessions from the steelmakers. The steel companies, realizing that they could wait until Eisenhower forced union members back to work, refused to make any such concessions. Ike was circumspect about the use of Taft-Hartley to end labor disputes. In a letter to McDonald on June 27, 1959, Ike stated: "In limiting this authority (use of Taft-Hartley) to emergencies, Congress, in my opinion, acted wisely..."

Eisenhower set in motion the Taft-Hartley machinery on October 7, 1959 and appointed a Board of Inquiry. However, Eisenhower limited the Board's mandate to clarifying the issues rather than recommending a settlement. Realizing that the strike could linger despite the use of the Taft-Hartley provisions, management offered a three-year contract with small improvements in pay, fringe benefits, and binding arbitration over Section 2(b). McDonald rejected the offer. He proposed a contract like his proposal of early July but reduced the union's wage and benefit demands and limited the contract to two rather than three years. Working from a plan devised by Goldberg, McDonald also proposed a nine-member committee consisting of three members from labor, management, and the public to study and resolve work-rule issues. Management rejected the new counter proposal (Tiffany, 1988). The Board of Inquiry issued its final report on October 19, 1959, declaring that there was zero chance of a negotiated settlement.

On October 20, 1959, the US Department of Justice petitioned the federal district court for Western Pennsylvania for a Taft-Hartley injunction ordering the USWA back to work. Goldberg and the USWA stated that the Taft-Hartley Act was unconstitutional, but the United States district court ruled for the government on October 21, 1959. The court agreed to a stay of the injunction until the matter was fully settled. The union appealed to the Third Circuit Court of Appeals in Philadelphia and lost again on October 27, 1959. The United States Supreme Court granted a writ certiorari, and the court date was set for November 3, 1959. On November 7, 1959, the 116th day of the strike, the Supreme Court upheld the appellate court's findings. In Steelworkers versus the United States, in an 8–1 decision, the court upheld the Taft-Hartley Act as constitutional. The US Supreme Court justices affirmed the district court's injunction and ordered the steelworkers back to work for an 80-day cooling-off period.

McDonald reluctantly ordered his members back to work, but productivity slowed due to extremely poor relationships between workers and managers. The Taft-Hartley Act required management to make a last offer and for union members to vote on this proposal. Management proposed minimal improvements in wages and benefits and the elimination of Section 2(b). The USWA members rejected the offer.

Figure 19: USWA Cleveland Local 1157 on Strike 1959.

Ike abhorred intervening in the strike. He would have much rather seen the industry leaders and labor resolve their differences without government intervention (Tiffany, 1988). In his memoir, *The White House Years, A Personal Account 1956-1961, Waging Peace*, (1965) Ike made clear his opposition to undue governmental interference in the economy: "Let the government fix wages, I argued, and it will next have to fix hours and work rules, moderate grievances, and finally set prices. Once it regulates wages and prices in major industries, it can run the entire economy and will soon run it for political, not economic, advantage... Moreover, government compulsion not only threatens economic liberty; it is also ineffective... federal intervention in labor-management disputes had often produced neither a satisfactory settlement nor prevented wage and price increases" (Eisenhower. 1965, p. 454).

The steel industry executives did believe that Ike would tip the scales in their favor. The election of Eisenhower in 1952 was welcomed by businesses in America. President Truman was seen as too much on the side of the unions. The president of Bethlehem Steel, Arthur B. Homer, had this to say in 1953 about the election of Ike: "The change in administration in Washington means that we should and will establish new relationships with government. It would seem, at present, that the basic economic philosophy of the Eisenhower regime is that the country should rely on free enterprise to continue prosperity and high living standards and that the government should act only as a stabilizer of desirable conditions-with a minimum of interference" (Tiffany, 1988, p. 103).

Generally, the industry wished for minimal interference on the part of the Eisenhower administration. Industry leaders seemed to fear that Ike's interference would result in wage increases that would be too generous to the steelworkers. In August 1959, Ike wrote George Humphrey, the chairman of National Steel to express his views on the strike: "What I am trying to say below is not to be interpreted as an effort to inject the government into the strike situation in the steel industry. I merely have put together in my own mind a 'formula' that makes sense to me. Admittedly, I have no intimate acquaintance with the steel business, but I do necessarily study daily a whole list of reports and I do have a good many indications of different convictions and opinions which have induced me to set forth the bare bones of what would seem to be fair to everybody" (Eisenhower, Galambos, and Van Ee, 2001, p. 1626). In his memoirs, *Waging Peace,* Ike gave a reason why he invoked the Taft-Hartley Act, leverage, which would give him several courses of action, as much as he abhorred government intervention in the strike.

At first, Ike believed that with the United States government offering third-party analysis of the data, labor and management might come together in mutual recognition of the facts. In January of 1959, Ike formed a Cabinet Committee on Price Stability for Economic Growth, whose main purpose was to conduct studies that would help prevent price increases. The Committee had little authority and subsequently had little impact. The Eisenhower administration refused to implement measures like price controls. Yet, Ike argued the decided upon contract should not compel prices to go up. In the 1988 book, *The Decline of American Steel, How Management, Labor, and Government Went Wrong,* the author Paul A. Tiffany sums up Ike's dilemma as one where Ike was "trapped between the poles of theory and pragmatism." Economic conservatism said hands-off to the economy. Political reality said some higher-level force must intervene to prevent the parties from harming the economy (Tiffany, 1988, p. 161).

Throughout most of 1959, Ike avoided a pronounced public role in the negotiations. He was, however, working behind the scenes in a major way with meetings, correspondence, and direction to his lieutenants such as Secretary of Labor Mitchell and VP Richard Nixon. Steel industry owners were dead set on preventing steel price hikes as part of the new contract. So, in April 1959, far ahead of the contract deadline, industry executives announced that they would only accept a one-year contract at existing pay and elimination of the cost-of-living escalator clause.

The existing United States economic slump appeared to give management a better hand in the negotiations. But there was fear among the steel industry customers that there could be a prolonged shortage of steel for their products - cars, buildings, infrastructure, washing machines, etc. Subsequently, there was a run on steel for the first two quarters of 1959, which resulted in record profits for the steel producers. Indeed, USC (the industry leader with the greatest market share) shipped more steel in the second quarter of 1959 than any previous quarter in its history. Thus, it was embarrassing for the steel company executives to deny USWA requests for wage hikes and increased benefits.

Both sides dug in for a long and bitter fight. McDonald was under great pressure to deliver a strong contract to USWA members. And R. Conrad Cooper, an executive VP at USC, and the industry negotiator for the 1959 contract, was expected to deliver to USA shareholders. By the end of June 1959, there was scant progress in the contract negotiations. On June 25, 1959, McDonald wrote Ike, "The steel negotiations are deadlocked," and he requested that Ike appoint an impartial fact-finding board to help with contract negotiations. On June 27, 1959, Ike rejected the idea, stating the Taft-Hartley Act called for a board like this only in emergencies. Ike communicated to McDonald by stating that the government should stay out of the negotiations and that the parties should resolve their disputes with free voluntary collective bargaining.

McDonald did postpone the strike date to July 15, 1959. McDonald decreased his demands for pay increases and agreed to a one-year contract. But the industry executives saw McDonald and the union in a compromised position. Cooper stated that the only way industry would negotiate was if the USW would agree to a complete wage freeze. And the only condition for granting even a small wage increase, Cooper stated, was that the USWA agree to modify a number of work rules - local working conditions, incentives, employee scheduling, and seniority. These were all factors that management wanted more control over to increase efficiency in the steel plants. The strike was called and on July 15, 1959, 511,000 steelworkers across the United States walked off the job for 116 days until November 7, 1959, when the US Supreme Court ordered them back to work under the 80-day cooling-off provision of the Taft-Hartley Act. "Giving the President a choice would put the contending parties in doubt as to the course he might elect and might induce them to resolve their differences sooner." (Eisenhower, 1965, p. 456).

In a letter from Charles M. White, the CEO and Chairman of Republic Steel, to Ike on July 20, 1959, White makes clear his displeasure at the prospect of the federal government interference in the outcome of the negotiations (...and by this I mean mostly the Labor Department.): "May I remind you that in each past instance when the government has intervened in steel industry labor disputes, the result has been a forced settlement of inflationary proportions." And in a letter dated September 8, 1959 to the 12 largest steel companies and McDonald at the USWA (as the strike reached its ninth week), Ike scolds and prods the principals for failing to make any progress in the negotiations: "It is disappointing and disheartening to our people that so little apparent progress toward settlement has been made thus far." Ike goes on to state; "The preservation of freedom is not an exclusive responsibility of government. Every individual to a greater or lesser extent shares that responsibility. This dispute is not a test of power. Compromising differences is a process with which I am familiar. I have seen far more difficult problems than the steel dispute resolved in far less time by people who spoke different languages and had diverse backgrounds. *Everything in my experience leads me to believe that where there is a will to agree on both sides, there is a way to agree"* (Italics Author) (Eisenhower, 1959, p. 644).

David McDonald, the president of the USWA immediately responded to Ike on September 9, 1959, and to the steel company executives by requesting a face-to-face private meeting where they could reach a settlement. The stalemate continued and Ike got more irritated with the parties. In a White House statement dated September 28, 1959, Ike's anger at the situation came through loud and clear: "I have this to say to you today on the steel strike. I am not going to try to assess any blame, but I am getting sick and tired of the apparent impasse in the settlement of this matter – and so are the American people. Free collective bargaining – the logical recourse of a free people in settling industrial disputes – has apparently broken down" (Eisenhower and Hagerty, 1959, p. 3).

In a letter from Republican Representative Francis E. Dorn September 23, 1959, U.S. House of Representative from New York's 12th district, Representative Dorn provides an assessment of the dispute as it was and makes the following recommendation for action to Ike: "All other reasonable courses having been exhausted, the only apparent alternative at this point is the use of the national emergency provisions of Taft-Hartley." Ike issued the Executive order that established the Board of Inquiry on October 9, 1959, stating "there was no hope for an early settlement" (Eisenhower and

Hagerty, 1959). It was October 19, 1959, that Ike sought an injunction to force the USWA back to work. "This is a sad day for the nation," Ike wrote (Eisenhower and Hagerty, 1959, p.3).

Ironically, neither the industry leaders nor the USWA wanted the injunction to return to work for a cooling-off period. McDonald, in quite a bit of hyperbole, claims that the single aim of the steel companies is to break the union. Arthur Goldberg General Counsel to the USWA, makes it clear that the USWA disagrees with Ike's contention that the steel strike constitutes a threat to the United States economy that merits the invocation of the Taft-Hartley Act. The USWA promptly challenged the injunction in court (Goldberg, United Steelworkers of America, and The Board of Inquiry, created by Executive Order, 9 October 1959).

On November 7, 1959, the US Supreme Court approved the injunction ordering the steelworkers back to work for 80 days. In a Memorandum-For the Record, written by Ike and dated November 9, 1959, Ike communicates that the crux of the dispute is the work rules. Ike states that management holds these rules antiquated and inefficient, and the rules price their products out of the market. The USWA labels any attempt to change these rules as trust-busting. Ike communicates that he and the US Department Labor Secretary Mitchell believes that management fails to understand how seriously the union membership takes this matter (Eisenhower, 1959).

The Report to the President - The 1959 Labor Dispute in The Steel Industry, submitted by the Board of Inquiry Executive Orders 10843 and 10848, October 19, 1959, sums up the situation well: "The union was not willing to discuss work rules provisions, which it held not to be negotiable. Since neither side would accept the preconditions of the other,

In Good Faith

effective negotiations could not proceed" (Board of Inquiry, 1959, p. 10).

Ike's exasperation intensified as illustrated by Ike stating that the "issue was whether or not reasonable men can get together and do this thing right" (Eisenhower, Galambos, and Van Ee 2001). Ike finally lays bare his anger when he asks in a personal letter to US Secretary of Treasury George Humphrey, "...what kind of thing the United States can do to protect itself against these disruptive strikes brought about by the selfishness and stupidity of both sides and which at the same time violate our principles of free economic practices" (Eisenhower, Galambos, and Van Ee, 2001, p. 1738).

This letter to George Humphrey was private, and it wasn't until the strike had gone on for two months that Ike showed a public interest by calling for action. Ike called the disputants to the White House in September of 1959 to meet with him separately. Still at an impasse, Ike initiated injunction proceedings by the appointment of the Board of Inquiry, and the Board submitted its report by October 17, 1959 stating: "As we submit this report, the parties have failed to reach an agreement and we see no prospects for an early cessation of the strike. *The Board cannot point to any single issue of any consequence whatsoever upon which the parties are in agreement"* (Italics Author) (Board of Inquiry, 1959, p. 16).

Ike directed VP Nixon and Labor Secretary Mitchell to have private meetings with the parties to seek a solution. The meetings were held at the Nixon home and the Waldorf Astoria Hotel in NYC. The meetings were brokered to provide a non-public, safer setting for the parties, unforced by the federal government to find a solution. These private meetings went on through December of 1959. Still, no resolution of the dispute (Eisenhower 1965). The USWA members were to vote on January 13, 1960 on the 'final' offer from management just before the Taft-Hartley injunction was set to expire. It was clear that the USWA members would reject the offer, and the strike would resume. The impasse continued. At this point, Secretary Mitchell called David McDonald and told him that the time had come, and he would have to break the line and come down. This time McDonald did reduce his demands.

In a Memorandum dated November 21, 1959, from Don Paarlberg, special assistant to the president for Economic Affairs, Mr. Paarlberg tallied letters to the White House on the issue of the strike, and out of 100 letters found that the letters were pro-management positions by 5 to 1. Apparently, there was a sense from the American people that the steelworkers had taken the strike too far and asked for too much. On Wednesday, December 30, 1959, all parties met again, and VP Nixon made it clear that if the strike continued, Congress would intervene. Nixon emphasized that Congress was controlled by the Democrats. The solution the Democrats would force would be one that was less favorable to management. This helped persuade management to accept the most recent labor offer (Eisenhower, 1965). The strike was settled on January 4, 1960. The settlement terms were unfavorable to the industry representatives. Industry would pay ~$.41/hour in increased wages and fringe benefits over thirty months, and management would abandon its attempts to change the work rules. David McDonald signed the settlement with enthusiasm. The United States steel industry executives signed the agreement without enthusiasm.

Ike believed that efforts to modernize work rules should be included in the agreement because they would result in more efficient steel making processes. Government economists

In Good Faith

concluded that the settlement would avoid inflation, and the next few months proved them correct. Ike's efforts failed to fully satisfy the parties, but this is often a sign of compromise. Ike found fault on all sides, and he failed to understand why the parties missed seeing the greater good of a settlement.

Management made a calculated gambit as they kept the work rules issue in their demands for a settlement. The work rules demands were portrayed as an attempt by management to break the USWA - that management was negotiating in bad faith. McDonald stated later that the industry, "... handed us an issue. I couldn't have written the script better myself" (Tiffany, 1988, p. 393). Management was insistent on the work rules issue because they believed that making manufacturing processes more efficient would help keep steel prices lower (and maintain profits) and offset the increases in pay and benefits that the USWA members would receive. This seems a reasonable assumption and request on the part of management in the contract negotiations. The final settlement included a thirty-month contract through June 1962. The terms favored labor as wages would be raised, benefits would be improved, the cost-of-living escalator would be extended, and the work rules issue was put off for further study.

Ike portrayed the settlement as a victory for voluntary and free bargaining. The truth was more complicated. Roger M. Blough, US Steel Chairman of the Board and CEO was clearly displeased with the outcome: "The union's refusal of our earlier offer created a serious deadlock. The union not only refused to bargain lower but after negotiating settlements in other industries, withdrew its previous offer and raised its demands very substantially" (Tiffany, 1988, p. 165).

The USWA gained more than it had expected. However, the gains were less than the 1956 contract negotiations. Management at US Steel told the Eisenhower administration after the settlement that the price of steel would remain stable at that time. Price increases were avoided, but the overall United States economy failed to improve, and the steel industry fell back to the low point it was experiencing in 1958. Public opinion was generally in favor of the compromise position of the Eisenhower administration. Secretary of Labor, James Mitchell, wrote Ike on February 18, 1959 that in a survey of 57 of the largest newspapers in the United States, 34 favored the position of the administration over the positions of the USWA or the industry owners. Twenty of the papers showed no strong preference for any of the positions (Mitchell, 1959).

Figure 20: Eisenhower and Press Secretary James Haggerty.

Ike repeated his insistence that the Federal Government should avoid interfering with the collective bargaining process. "Federal Government should not interfere with the actual bargaining process...the final settlement should be and will be made by the parties themselves" (Eisenhower and

McDonald, 1959). These statements by Ike were both canny and dubious. They were canny since Ike was clear that his administration would keep its hand off the scales in this dispute - especially considering past strikes where the federal government did tip the scales in favor of the unions. The statements were dubious as Ike and his administration were working furiously behind the scenes to end the dispute as soon as possible without a hike in the price of steel that would further existing inflation.

Ever the diplomat and seeking impartiality, Ike writes to Roger Blough, CEO of US Steel Corporation on February 3, 1960, after the strike has ended: "I know that the complications were many and that tempers often frayed and patience exhausted. But it is a tribute to you and your associates – and of course, the union too – that finally the matter was resolved without undue damage to our country" (Eisenhower, Blough, 1960, p. 1).

Hardline American conservatives were angry that Nixon intervened and brought about a resolution that favored the USWA. Ideological conservatives such as William F. Buckley, Jr. denounced the settlement and denounced Ike's "middle way" Republicanism as weak and ineffectual. As a result of the added labor costs to produce their product, and a subsequent decline in profits, the steel companies tried to increase their prices in the early 1960s. President John F. Kennedy ordered the Justice Department and the FBI to threaten the steel companies with arrest for criminal violations of antitrust laws.

The subsequent years and decades would see a steady decline in the United States steel industry leaving American communities and state and local economies devastated. The intransigence of both labor and management would ultimately end in tragedy for the US steel industry - two very powerful entities seeking their own narrow, self-interest at the expense of one another, and US economic health.

Ike was an honest broker in the arbitration of the 1959 US Steel Strike. He refused to take sides in the bargaining agreement. Ike invoked the Taft-Hartley Act in the hopes that this would force the two sides to bargain *in good faith*. In refusing to compromise, both sides ultimately lost in the negotiations. In negotiation, it is important to have a long view, focus on the issues at hand and look to the future, while avoiding a zero-sum game. Ike coerced the parties to meet for negotiation. "The exact methods of the negotiations were unimportant. What was important was a fair settlement" (Eisenhower, 1965, p. 457).

Throughout the 1959 Steel Strike negotiations, Ike avoided proscriptive settlement solutions with either labor or management. Instead, he regularly asked how he could help - what type of resources the US Federal Government could provide. Ike believed that collective bargaining was the right and responsibility of a free people. Ike sometimes communicated his anger that the labor and management were very small-minded in their demands and were selfish. This resulted in the strike lasting so long, with devastating immediate, short-term, and long-term effects on the well-being of American families and the United States economy.

Ike attempted to bring the parties together on mutual interests, with little success. Management was willing to hold out for lower wages and updated work rules, while labor was entrenched with the opposite demands. Ultimately, it was the threat of a more liberal Congress intervening on behalf of labor that forced management to accept most of the demands of labor.

In Good Faith

Ike focused on ending the strike and returning the United States economy to a healthier state. However, the two sides were recalcitrant in their positions and seemed to have little heed for the damage that the strike was doing to the US economy. Although labor and management goals were generally aligned - more steel production, more steelworkers employed - each side saw the other as the enemy, unable to agree upon shared goals. The result of the 1959 Steel Strike negotiations was attrition for the US steel industry and the US economy.

Lou Villaire

Chapter 6:
The U2 Incident of 1960: Count to Ten Before You Say Anything

On May 1, 1960, a United States U2 Spy Plane (Dragon Lady) was shot down over Sverdlovsk, Russia, inside Soviet Union (USSR) airspace. President Eisenhower had approved the design, construction, and reconnaissance flights of the high-altitude U2 Spy Plane several years before. At that time, Eisenhower was prescient, stating that he would rue the day that he approved the manufacture of this plane and authorized its flights. Ike was concerned that the Soviets would shoot down one of these spy planes. The U2 plane flew at 70,000 feet, taking pictures of Soviet military installations, among other things.

Figure 21: United States U2 Spy Plane, Circa 1955.

Details were uncertain but seemed clear that the U2 spy plane was shot down. However, the United States lacked communication with the thirty-year-old pilot, Gary Powers, and could not confirm the downing of the plane. At first, Eisenhower publicly denied that the U2 was a spy plane, but rather, it was a weather information gathering plane that had flown off course.

The idea for the U2 was originally brought to the US Air Force by Clarence L. (Kelly) Johnson, a Lockheed vice-president, and its chief designer. Johnson had the idea of putting a jet engine inside of a glider. The huge wings would support the weight of the aircraft while still being very light. Being so light would allow the plane to operate at very high altitudes (Ambrose, 1981). The first official flight of the U2 was August 1, 1955, when the spy plane left Wiesbaden, West Germany, and flew directly into Soviet territory, first over Moscow and then over Leningrad. Overall, the U2 program was a great success for the United States CIA. The U2 program was later taken over by the US Air Force. The U2 program continues today, gathering intelligence for the US government.

The U2 program had its origins in early 1954 when Ike appointed a "Surprise Attack Panel." Ike was anxiously concerned about the possibility of a surprise attack on the United States by the Soviets. The Surprise Attack Panel had three subcommittees. One of the subcommittees was concerned with intelligence gathering. The main members of the intelligence subcommittee were Edwin H. Land and Edward Purcell. Edwin H. Land was the inventor of the Polaroid camera and CEO of the Polaroid Corporation. Edward Purcell was a professor of physics at Harvard University and a winner of the Nobel Prize in Physics in 1952 (Bissell, Jr., Soapes, and Edwin, 1967, 1976).

Land had learned that Lockheed Corporation had recently proposed a high-altitude plane (70,000 feet) to the US Air Force (Ambrose, 1981). The US Air Force passed on the proposal. Land concluded that the US Air Force made a mistake in failing to pursue the project. Land and Purcell went to Allen Dulles, Director of the CIA, and convinced him to pursue the U2 project. Dulles took the project to Ike, and Ike approved the program. Shortly thereafter, CIA Officer Richard Bissell Jr. became the project director for the U2 program. The program moved quickly. Bissell had this to say about the program's chaotic start: "Nobody had really worked out how anything was going to be done. Nobody knew where the money was coming from. Nobody knew who would procure the aircraft. Nobody had even given any thought to where it could be developed, where flight testing could be done, where people could be trained or by whom, and who would fly it or anything" (Ambrose, 1990, p. 268-269).

Bissell and Dulles determined that the funding for the U2 program would come from the CIA Reserve Fund, which could be released by the president or the director of the budget. Covert procurement of the U2 development funding was accomplished. Lockheed began the highly secret construction of the aircraft at the Skunk Works hangar in Burbank, CA. Pratt-Whitney built the engine, and Hycon built the cameras. The project moved with incredible speed. Within months, by early 1954, the plane was ready for testing. The first U2 cost the American taxpayers 3 million dollars (~$30,000,000 in 2022 dollars). Ray Cile, a CIA analyst charged with gathering information on the USSR, said that the plane, "Looked more like a kite built around a camera than an airplane" (Ambrose, 1990, p. 269).

The imaging technology of the U2 spy plane was exceptional for its time. The plane could fly as high as 70,000 feet and take photos with a resolution that could show the lines of parking spaces in a parking lot. The U2 took photos that were of better resolution than was available from satellites at that time. Shortly after the test flights, Bissell ordered 22 U2s from Lockheed (Ambrose, 1981). Ike insisted that the whole operation be conducted through the CIA as a civilian intelligence-gathering operation rather than a military operation. In June of 1955, Ike authorized an initial flight period of ten days total. In those ten days, Bissell was able to run a total of six missions. There were some technical restrictions with the U2 flights. Namely, the U2 could only take good photos during times of clear weather. U2 flights were inherently dangerous.

The May 1, 1960 crash of the U2 was one of several mishaps with the plane. On September 17, 1956, a U2 crashed near Kaiserslautern, West Germany, killing the pilot, Howard Carey, a Lockheed employee. Then, on April 4, 1957, a U2 crashed in Northwest Nevada killing the pilot, Robert L. Sieker, also a Lockheed employee. In all, five US Strategic Air Command (SAC) U2 pilots were killed through 1958.

The U2 flights brought back exceptional intelligence, including information on airfields, aircraft missile testing, nuclear weapons storage, submarine production, atomic production, and aircraft use. The quality of the U2 photos was extraordinary. A U2 was once sent over China to check a report that the Maoists had a vertical ballistic missile ready for launch. The U2 took photos of the site and found the ballistic missile was actually a tall medieval tower (Beschloss, 1986).

The Soviets were unhappy with the repeated U2 flights into the territory of the USSR. The Soviets sent private communication to the US government protesting the U2 flights. The USSR was tracking the U2 flights with its radar. It turns out that the Soviets had better radar than the United States. Ike then told Bissell to slow down on the flights. It was some months before another flight was authorized. Indeed, from this point on, Ike personally authorized flights on a case-by-case basis. After that, Ike was involved directly even in the flight paths of the U2. For example, during the Suez Crisis of 1956, Ike asked Bissell to have the U2 complete flights over Syria, Egypt, and Israel to investigate whether the Russians were moving airplanes into Egypt. During the Hungarian Revolution of October/November of 1956, the United States conducted overflights with the U2 to determine the movements of the Red Army (Ambrose, 1990). Secretary of State, Dulles, told Ike that the United States was in trouble due to all these overflights, and the president responded by saying that he was thinking about a "complete stoppage of the whole business." However, the flights were too valuable. Bissell now had about 500 personnel involved in the flights, and the United States had the capability to monitor just about any place in the world with a 24-hour notice. The United States was even spying on its allies. Specifically, the United States wanted to know more about the French, English, and Israeli invasion of Egypt. On October 30, 1956, the U2 pilot, Gary Powers, photographed clouds of black smoke in the Sinai Desert - the first signs of the Israeli invasion of Egypt.

In another international incident in September of 1958, the Premier of the People's Republic of China, Chou En-lai, warned the leader of the Republic of China, Chiang Kai-shek, that if he refused to abandon the islands of Quemoy and Matsu, that the People's Republic of China would invade Formosa (now Taiwan). U2 flights revealed nothing. Ike famously went on US national TV and announced to the world that there would be no invasion. The U2 program brought exceptional intelligence, which helped prevent international conflict (Ambrose, 1990). In fact, the U2 program saved US taxpayers billions of dollars because Ike was able to show evidence that a US military build-up was unnecessary. Ike's *New Look* defense policy restrained military spending with a greater emphasis on expanding world economic interdependence to help avoid military conflict. By holding down military spending and inflation, Ike was able to balance the US budget. Ike believed that arms races were senseless and that an arms race in a nuclear age was insane (Ambrose, 1990).

One of the many facts that the U2 flights proved was that the 'missile gap' between the USSR and the United States was a fallacy. Indeed, one of the central claims of John F. Kennedy's US presidential campaign of 1960 was that there was a missile gap between the United States and the USSR and that his administration would address this gap. Ike claimed that this gap was non-existent. Ike was correct - this he knew primarily from U2 flights. When Ike left office in January 1961, the United States had about 200 Inter-Continental Ballistic Missiles (ICBMs). By the time President Kennedy was assassinated, on November 22, 1963, the United States had 1000 ICBMs, and the number was growing every day. Years later, Kennedy's own Secretary of Defense, Robert McNamara, also stated that there had been no such thing as a missile gap (Ambrose, 1981).

Shortly after Ike approved the U2 flights, he unveiled his ambitious program of detente with the Soviets that Ike called Open Skies. Ike presented the Open Skies program to the world at the July 18, 1955, Geneva Peace Conference. The Conference was attended by the United States, USSR, France, and the UK. The goal of the Conference was to begin conversations on peace, especially global security. One of the world's greatest fears was a surprise nuclear attack (Ambrose, 1990). At the Geneva Peace Conference, Ike made the extraordinary proposal that the USSR could build airfields on US soil so that the Soviets could monitor US installations. The United States would expect the same from the Soviets. Ike was sincere in this proposal, but the Soviets turned him down, claiming that the proposal was a US plot to spy on Mother Russia (Ambrose, 1990). On April 6, 1960, Ike approved more U2 flights into Russian territory. But Ike was very apprehensive. The next day Ike told Bissell that he had changed his mind. "As the world is going now, there seems no hope for the future unless we can make some progress in the negotiation. It is already four years since the Geneva meeting" (Beschloss, 1986, p. 703).

Ike was very concerned about the "terrible propaganda impact" of a plane crash. "We cannot in the present circumstance afford the revulsion of world opinion against the United States that might occur." Ike knew the necessity of gathering valuable intelligence, and he did think that the information was worth the political costs (Beschloss, 1986, p. 703). Ike was repeatedly concerned about the U2 overflights and often asked the CIA what would happen if one of the U2 planes were caught. The CIA continued to respond – "it hasn't happened yet." The US Secretary of Defense, Neil H. McElroy, humbly stated that it was "far easier for Cabinet officers to recommend this activity than for the President to authorize it." The CIA, the Pentagon, and the Joint Chiefs of Staff were back to ask for more U2 flights (Ambrose, 1990, p. 529).

It appears that Ike approved and conducted the U2 program under the assumption that he and the US government would have plausible deniability if one of the planes and or pilots were captured by the USSR. Plausible deniability is a term defined by the US National Security Council to describe US government involvement that is "not evident to authorized persons and if uncovered, the government can plausibly disclaim any responsibility for them." The CIA and the Joint Chiefs of Staff convinced Ike that if one of the U2 planes were downed, any evidence of espionage was unrecoverable. The U2 planes were equipped with self-destruct mechanisms - namely 4-5 pounds of cyclonite explosive (aka RDX, which is more explosive and powerful than TNT).

However, the self-destruct mechanisms (including a cyanide pill for the pilot) required manual actions by the pilot to initiate. U2 pilots, of course, had a choice to take the cyanide or not. It was their option, and not a good option. Richard Bissell told Ike that the U2 was so fragile that it would pretty much break up in an accident. Bissell went on to say that the chances of a pilot surviving a U2 mishap were one chance in a million. Even though, a few U2s had already crashed outside of Russia, and the pilots had survived. All the U2 planes were equipped with ejection seats, which did permit escape. There was supposedly a 70-second delay before the set-off of the RDX after the pilot had activated the seat ejection mechanism of the U2 (Beschloss, 1986).

A Top-Secret Memo dated April 25, 1960, from A.J. Goodpaster said this of the fateful flyover of the U2 by Gary Powers: "After checking with the President, I informed Mr. Bissell that one additional operation may be undertaken, provided it is carried out before May 1. No operation is to be carried out after May 1, 1960" (Ambrose, 1981, p. 569). This fateful order led to the downing of the U2 by the Soviets. It is worthwhile to note that May 1st was a Soviet national holiday (May Day), and there would be very little air traffic. This would make it even more likely that the U2 would be spotted in Soviet airspace.

In Good Faith

One of the greatest aspirations that Ike had as president was international arms control (Beschloss, 1986). Ike had experienced war firsthand, and he sought non-military solutions. Ike believed that international trade was the key to peace, as opposed to the Mutual Assured Destruction (MAD) posed by nuclear armaments. In his famous Cross of Iron speech Ike stated: "Every gun that is made, every warship launched, every rocket fired signifies, in the final sense, a theft from those who hunger and are not fed, those who are cold and are not clothed. This world in arms is not spending money alone" (Eisenhower, Chance for Peace Speech, 1961).

In March of 1960, Ike told British Prime Minister, Harold Macmillan, he wanted to capitalize on the Soviet fears that China would soon develop nuclear weapons. Ike was very keen on reaching some type of test ban at the Paris Summit in May of 1960. But Ike knew that the U2 flights put all this goodwill, and his reputation for honesty, at stake. Ike said that the decision to fly the U2 planes at different times was "always an agonizing question" (Beschloss, 1986). Ike knew that the valuable US intelligence gathering of the U2 spy plane was balanced against diplomatic efforts with the USSR. What Ike neglected to appreciate is that Khrushchev's credibility as a leader within the Soviet Union would suffer if US spy planes were discovered over the USSR. Ike remained reluctant to continue the U2 flights. He wanted to wait for the operation of the Corona satellite. Ike said that the U2 flights were an undue provocation. Ike considered what he would do if he were in the place of Khrushchev. Ike thought "nothing would make him request authority to declare war more quickly than the violation of our air space by Soviet aircraft" (Hitchcock, 2018, p. 468).

Ike considered the decision to continue the U2 flights as "Such a decision is one of the most soul-searching questions to become before a president" (Hitchcock, 2018, p. 460). By 1960 the Soviets had improved their ability to shoot down a U2 plane. Richard Bissell, co-director of the CIA's National Reconnaissance Office, assured Ike if a Soviet missile were launched at a United States U2 plane, "it would be a near miss rather than a hit" (Beschloss, 1986). Bissell, of course, was wrong in his assertion. The single-seat U2 spy aircraft, flown by pilot Francis Gary Powers, was hit by an S-75 Dvina (SA-2 Guideline) surface-to-air missile, and the plane crashed near Sverdlovsk (today's Yekaterinburg) (Hitchcock, 2018, p. 462).

Bissell knew that the April 9, 1960 flight of the U2, which brought back detailed photos of the Soviet missile sites in Semipalatinsk and Tyuratam (what is now Kazakhstan), was tracked by the Russians even before it entered Soviet airspace. Bissell failed to tell Ike about this incident.

Figure 22: The Flight Path of the Gary Powers Piloted United States U2 Surveillance Plane, May 1, 1960.

It was just before 9 AM Moscow Standard Time on May 1, 1960, when the Soviet SA-2 Guideline surface-to-air missile exploded right behind the U2 aircraft that Gary Powers was piloting. Powers was about 70,000 feet up when the

In Good Faith

explosion of the missile shook the U2. Powers lost control of the plane as it began to break apart, going into a downward spiral. Powers ejected from the plane and opened his parachute. In the chaos, Powers failed to detonate the explosives that would have destroyed the aircraft. Powers, along with large chunks of the aircraft, went to the ground. The Soviets apprehended Powers, and shortly thereafter Powers was on his way to the Lubyanka Prison in Moscow. It was May Day in the USSR, a national holiday celebrating the Russian Workers Revolution. Khrushchev was attending the Moscow May Day Parade when he was informed by the head of the USSR air defenses that the Powers' plane had been shot down.

Gary Powers had flown twenty-seven U2 missions in the previous four years. He was an experienced pilot. His logbook had the notations "May 1, 1960. Sortie (a combat mission of a single aircraft) Number 4154. Takeoff 0126 GMT (Greenwich Mean Time) [6:26 a.m. local time], delayed ½ hour" In front of Powers in the U2 cockpit was his map on which was traced a red and blue line showing a 3,788-mile flight from Peshawar, Pakistan to Bodo, Norway. This flight would take Powers 2,919 miles, at about 70,000 feet above the earth through USSR airspace past Stalingrad (now Volgograd), Aralsk (in now Kazakhstan), Sverdlovsk (now the City Yekaterinburg), Kirov (in Western Russia), Archangel (aka Arkhangelsk, in the North of European Russia), and Murmansk (the NW part of Russia). Flying about 13 miles above the earth, the temperature can be as low as 100 degrees below zero.

Powers was known on his radio as "Puppy 68." As Powers approached the border of the USSR, he switched on the device that created an artificial static for enemy radar. At this point, his plane was headed straight toward the Aral Sea and Tyuratam (now Kazakhstan), which was the Soviet

155

equivalent of the US Cape Canaveral in Florida. The primary purpose of the May 1, 1960, U2 flight was to photograph the construction of any intercontinental ballistic missile sites at Tyuratam. Powers was carrying one of the world's most powerful cameras. It was a 944.7-millimeter lens that looked out of seven holes in the bottom of the U2 plane. The camera would take 4,000 paired pictures of a 125-mile wide, 2,174-mile-long strip of the USSR.

Soviet Minister of Defense Rodion Malinovsky had called Khrushchev at 5 AM, the morning of May 1, 1960, to inform Khrushchev that a United States U2 reconnaissance plane had passed the border of Afghanistan and was heading toward the city of Sverdlovsk (Yekaterinburg). Khrushchev told Malinovsky to shoot down the plane, "by whatever means he could." Malinovsky told Khrushchev that he had already given the order, "If our anti-aircraft units can just keep their eyes open and stop yawning long enough, I'm sure we'll knock the plane down" (Khrushchev, 2013, p. 443). By the time the news of the downed U2 plane reached Ike, he was at Camp David, but he immediately boarded a helicopter back to the White House. Bissell later said that he "felt a sense of disaster about the entire affair." The CIA was "not well prepared for what happened" (Hitchcock, 2018, p. 462).

The Soviets had been enduring these flights for several years, and according to Khrushchev, "We were more infuriated and disgusted every time a violation occurred." And after the downing of the U2 over Sverdlovsk, Khrushchev felt triumphant and wrote in his memoirs, "We were sick and tired of these unpleasant surprises, sick and tired of being subjected to these indignities. They (the US) were making these flights to show our impotence. Well, we weren't impotent any longer" (Khrushchev, 2013, p. 443). It seems that Ike and the CIA failed to appreciate the extent of the Soviet anger at these repeated violations of Soviet airspace.

In his memoirs, Khrushchev recounts an old Russian folk proverb that is apt in the situation where Ike had repeatedly approved the U2 flights, sometimes against his better judgment. The proverb says no matter how many times you fetch water from the well in the same pitcher, sooner or later, the day comes when the pitcher breaks (Khrushchev, 2013). Khrushchev made his announcement regarding the downed U2 flight to the world on May 5, 1960, at the Supreme Soviet. Khrushchev spoke passionately about US militarism and aggression in the world. Khrushchev blamed the American Pentagon and the US militarists' drive for world domination for the U2 flights, and the violation of Soviet airspace (Ambrose, 1990).

Khrushchev appeared to have executed his plan quite well. Evidently, Khrushchev had previously proposed the plan to the Supreme Soviet. In his memoirs, Khrushchev recounts his plan: "I would make a speech at the session and inform the Supreme Soviet that the Americans had violated the sovereignty of our State; I would announce that the plane had been shot down, but - and this was important - I would not reveal that the pilot had been captured alive and was in our hands. Our intention here was to confuse the government circles of the United States. If the Americans thought the pilot was dead, they would keep putting out the story that perhaps the plane had accidentally strayed off course and been shot down in the mountains on the Soviet side of the border" (Khrushchev, 1974, p. 446).

Ironically, the instructions given to the U2 pilots by the CIA if they were captured, "Was to adopt a cooperative attitude toward their captors [and feel] perfectly free to tell the full truth about their mission except for certain specifications of the aircraft" (Wise and Ross, 1962, p. 19). Indeed, Powers did just this, revealing most of the details of his mission. Powers went even further and expressed remorse for his mission directly to the Soviet people and the world. Powers communicated that he thought his mission had ultimately harmed the cause of world peace.

When Khrushchev announced to the world that the Soviets had shot down a US reconnaissance plane that violated Soviet airspace well into Soviet territory, Ike's advisors suggested that Ike make another statement immediately. Ike voiced serious doubts about issuing another statement. But he was persuaded, and the US State Department issued a second false statement, consistent with the first that a United States U2 weather research plane based in Adana had been missing since May 1, 1960 (Eisenhower, 1965, p. 550). Ike was at his Gettysburg farm when he read the statement claiming that the plane had probably invaded Soviet airspace, but that the pilot was unauthorized to do so. At this time, Ike said that this false statement "might prove to be a mistake." It got worse for Ike. Khrushchev went on to announce at the Supreme Soviet that the surviving U2 pilot admitted "his mission had been to penetrate deeply into the Soviet Union" (Eisenhower, 1965, p. 550).

There was another misrepresentation of the U2 incident that Ike rejected. Ike could claim that he was the "victim of overzealous subordinates." Ike could then dismiss Dulles and/or Bissell as acting improperly. Ike refused this story not only because it was untrue but also because it portrayed him as a leader out of touch with his own government. Ike believed that this story would play into the hands of the USSR. On May 5, 1960, both the US State Department and NASA issued conflicting statements about the U2 flight. The State Dept. stayed with the original cover story. However, NASA released additional lies about the incident. NASA stated that the U2 was one of 10 "flying weather laboratories" that NASA operated around the world, and that the U2 was a civilian aircraft operated by a civilian scientist pilot and refrained from taking any photographs. Khrushchev disproved these lies by producing parts of the aircraft, including cameras, as well as finally producing the U2 pilot Powers, who admitted to working for the United States CIA. However, Ike and his staff tried to continue the lie by stating that the U2 was a civilian aircraft and "there was no authorization for any such flight" (Ambrose, 1990, p. 286).

After sticking with their phony story for several days, the US Secretary of State, Christian Herter, recommended to Ike that the United States come clean on the affair. The story they decided to tell was an unapologetic one where Ike clearly communicated that he had a duty as the US president to protect the American people from a Soviet surprise attack. Intelligence gathering operations by US spy planes over Soviet airspace are part of that charge. Ike said in his memoirs, "I felt anything but apologetic." Ike went on in his memoirs to state: "My acknowledgment of responsibility for espionage activities was practically unprecedented in history, but so were the circumstances. Francis Gary Powers was no individual traveler sneaking across borders between guards and living in concealed garrets in the land of a potential enemy;... but when the world can entertain not the slightest doubt of the facts there is no point in trying to evade the issue" (Eisenhower, 1965, p. 550).

According to journalists David Wise and Thomas B. Ross in their 1962 book entitled *The U2 Affair*, it was the first time in the 184-year history of the United States that the US government had stated publicly that it had lied, that it had committed espionage, and that it had violated the territorial integrity of another sovereign nation. The authors continue,

"It was the first time in American history that a president had taken personal, public responsibility for conducting espionage" (Wise and Ross, 1960, p. 108).

Figure 23: Khrushchev viewing wreckage of the U2.

However, in acknowledging that the United States had invaded Soviet airspace with the U2 (more than once) the president was telling the Soviets that the United States had a right to do this. Khrushchev said this sounded "as though Eisenhower were boasting arrogantly about what the United States could do and would do." And in discussing espionage activities in general, Ike goes on to state in the footnotes: "Espionage was distasteful but vital. And, as I remarked later to the group of bipartisan Congressional leaders, the decision was mine. One had to weigh the risks, keep the knowledge in as few hands as possible, and accept the consequences if something went wrong. There is no glory in this business, if it *is* successful, it cannot be told" (Eisenhower, 1965, p. 551 Footnotes).

Ike told his staff after he came clean on the U2 affair to the world: "We will now just have to endure the storm with everyone realizing that it was I personally and rightly so-who would do the enduring" (Eisenhower, 1965, p. 552). Republican Senator Hugh Scott of Pennsylvania stated publicly that the loss of the United States U2 plane had violated the 11th Commandment "thou shall not get caught" (Beschloss, 1986). The response from major news outlets was mixed, but the embarrassment and anger were communicated. The San Francisco Chronicle wrote "Moral Leadership of US Harmed." The Washington Post wrote, "This Country Was Caught with Jam on Its Hands." The St. Louis Post-Dispatch referred to President Eisenhower as a "barefaced liar." James Reston of the New York Times accused Ike of removing himself from key decisions. And Walter Lippmann of the New York Herald Tribune wrote "It seems as if the country has been humiliated by absentmindedness in the highest quarters of the government" (Hitchcock, 2018, p. 466). Ike told a friend that when a president loses his credibility "he has lost his greatest strength" (Beschloss, 1986, p. 287).

On the morning of May 9, 1960, Ike returned from a breakfast with Republican congressmen. According to Ike's personal secretary, Ann Whitman, Ike arrived at the White House very depressed, and famously stated to Ann Whitman, "I would like to resign" (Beschloss, 1986, p. 289). Later that day, at a US National Security Council meeting, Ike stated the following about the U2 flights: "Of course, one had to expect that the thing would fail at one time or another. But that it had to be such a boo-boo and that we would be caught with our pants down was rather painful. We will just have to endure the storm" (Beschloss, 1986, p. 290). Although Ike was personally "enduring the storm" over the U2 incident. Privately, Ike was displeased with some of his staff, especially CIA Director Allen Dulles.

There was some begrudging apology from the United States to the USSR for having Powers shot down in the U2 above Soviet airspace. But the surveillance would continue. Vice President Nixon, in a late-night interview with host David Susskind, stated that the United States would continue the U2 flights because the flights help protect the United States "and our allies." Khrushchev saw an opportunity to use the United States U2 pilot to his advantage. The Soviets interrogated Powers for days, and Powers told the Soviets about the flight. Khrushchev had this to say about Powers: "However well-trained Powers may have been, he didn't do as he was told. His willpower wasn't strong enough to overcome his desire to go on living; he just couldn't bring himself to commit suicide" (Khrushchev, 1974, p. 445).

Apologies to the descendants of pilot Gary Powers, but would the outcome of the U2 incident of May 1, 1960 be different had Powers been killed during the shooting down of the U2? Probably not, because his identity and mission would have eventually been revealed. Powers, like other U2 pilots, was offered an 'L' pill, which stood for lethal. This pill contained cyanide and was in a glass capsule. If the U2 pilot wished to commit suicide, he could crush the capsule between his teeth (Whittell, 2010, p. 69).

Ike warned the public and reporters at a press conference, "We must not be distracted from the real issues of the day by what an incident or a symptom of the world situation today." To shift focus from the U2 to the Paris Summit, "The real issues are the ones we will be working on at the Summit-disarmament, search for solutions Germany and Berlin and a whole range of East-West relations" (US Department of State Bulletin, Vol. 42, p 852).

According to Susan Eisenhower, the granddaughter of Ike, and an expert in US/Russian relations, there are a few theories as to why Khrushchev had the U2 shot down just weeks before the Paris Peace Summit. Susan Eisenhower claims that in one theory Khrushchev knew that the summit would fail at its goals, so stopping it could be blamed on the Americans. Another theory was that Eisenhower's world travels had intimidated Khrushchev. Still another theory stated that Soviet hard-liners were upset by Khrushchev's visit to the United States (Eisenhower, 2020).

Throughout his presidency, Ike sought better relations with the USSR along with efforts to reduce the world's nuclear arsenal. But Ike was clear-eyed about his interactions with the Soviets. He was also confident in his knowledge that the United States was superior to the USSR in its military power. But Ike also understood that the United States had an inherent disadvantage in its negotiations with a totalitarian power like the USSR. Namely, Ike understood that the United States was negotiating in good faith, and the USSR had less incentive to do so. Ike had no intention of humiliating Khrushchev at the Paris Summit. In an excellent assessment of the U2 Affair *Mayday: Eisenhower, Khrushchev, and the U2 Affair* historian, Michael R. Beschloss, states: "To the extent that the U2 was responsible, it is difficult to escape the conclusion that both the American and Soviet governments participated in the shattering of a detente" (1986, p. 428).

Despite all the anti-capitalist rhetoric, the United States was held by Russians in a venerable position, especially General Eisenhower. During WWII, the United States and the USSR were allies in defeating the Nazis. Ike had a strong relationship with Soviet General Georgy Zhukov. Zhukov led some of the greatest battles in WWII, including the battle of Stalingrad. Eisenhower and Zhukov went on to tour the Soviet Union together in the immediate aftermath of the victory over Germany. Joseph Stalin said that it was because of Ike that the Soviets took Berlin. It was the Soviet Army that first liberated Berlin. Khrushchev was also fond of Ike. Khrushchev visited the United States in September of 1959 at the invitation of Ike. Ike's scheduled to visit the USSR in the Spring of 1960, was canceled because of the U2 Affair.

Khrushchev blamed the militarists in Ike's administration for the U2 incident. Khrushchev did appear to want the Paris Summit to take place. Khrushchev stated, "I do not doubt President Eisenhower's desire for peace" (Beschloss, 1986, p. 57). But Khrushchev very much wanted an apology from Ike for the U2 incident. When Ike arrived in Paris, Khrushchev made three demands of Ike before Khrushchev would permit the Summit to continue. Khrushchev demanded that Ike apologize for the Powers' flight, discipline those parties responsible for the flights, and stop any more U2 flights.

When Ike heard these demands, he was angry, and he said that he would be damned if he would condemn or apologize for an activity the USSR and all other nations participated in. Khrushchev used the U2 Affair to the fullest extent possible to manipulate the Paris Summit. Khrushchev stated: "I cannot be among the participants in negotiations when one of them has made perfidy the basis of its policy toward the Soviet Union" (Davis, 1967, p. 414). In a telling display of bravado showing hurt and humiliation, Khrushchev broke protocol at the beginning of the Summit by being the first to speak. As per historic guidelines, heads of state were allowed to speak first - both Khrushchev and Macmillan were prime ministers, so Ike was expected to speak first, but

Khrushchev jumped in and began his condemnation of the United States for the U2 flight. "Just a minute," said Khrushchev, "I asked first, and I have something to say."

Khrushchev started his hours-long monologue as Ike was just set to speak, with the words "a provocative act." And the air in the room heated up. Ike's neck was getting red, his face became flush, and his lips were set in anger. When Ike finally had the chance to respond, he controlled his anger and stated that the U2 flights "had no aggressive intent but rather were to assure the safety of the United States and the free world against surprise attack" (US Congress, 1960, p. 46). And Ike went on to condemn the same activity by the Soviets "As is well known, not only the United States but most other countries are constantly the targets of elaborate and persistent espionage of the Soviet Union" (US Congress, p. 55). Ike continued to announce publicly for the first time that the U2 flights over Russia would end.

Khrushchev then revoked his previous invitation for Ike to visit the Soviet Union in the summer of 1960. Ike told Khrushchev that he was unapologetic for his actions to protect the national security of Americans, but he had already suspended the U2 flights. Ike went on to state the United States was willing to engage the Russians in bilateral talks either at the Paris Summit or elsewhere. Khrushchev walked out of the conference (Hitchcock, 2018). At the Paris Peace Summit, Khrushchev claimed, "American flights over Soviet territory have been and remain the calculated policy of the United States" (Beschloss, 1986, p. 323). Rodion Malinovsky, Minister of Defense, of the Soviet Union, summed up the views of the USSR when he questioned, as the Summit began: "How is it possible to productively negotiate and examine the questions facing the Conference when the US government and the President himself have not only failed to condemn this provocative act...but declared that such acts will continue" (p. 323).

Khrushchev continued with his condemnation of Ike, the US, and the U2 incident: "We do not understand what devil pushed you into doing this provocative act to us just before the Conference. If there had been no incident, we would have come here in friendship and the best possible atmosphere. I recall that at Camp David, the President and I said to call each other 'my friend.' Now, these two friends have collided in the skies. Our rocket shot the plane down. Is this good friendship? As God is my witness, I come with clean hands and a pure soul" (Beschloss, 1986, p. 326).

Participants of the Summit sought to get the meeting back on track, but the Soviets prevented it. Later in life, Khrushchev explained his view on the Summit and the Soviet position: "We had to present an ultimatum to the United States. They would have to apologize for the insult and injury done to our country. We would have to demand that the president take back his statement asserting the right of the United States to make spy flights over foreign territory, something no sovereign state could permit" (Khrushchev, 1974, p. 451).

Khrushchev (who was known for his hyperbole) had the following uncorroborated description of the opening events at the Paris Summit in his memoirs: "My interpreter, Comrade Sukhodrev, told me he noticed, while reading the English translation of my statement, that Eisenhower turned to his Secretary of State, Mr. Herter, and said, 'Well, why not? Why don't we go ahead and make a statement of apology?' Herter said no - and he said it in such a way, with such a grimace on his face, that he left no room for argument on the issue. As a result, Eisenhower refused to apologize" (Khrushchev, 1974, p. 454). This incident, as described by Khrushchev, is uncorroborated by any other observers of the

Summit. Khrushchev writes in his memoirs that: "...he (Ike) knew it was possible for him to give us the apology and assurances we were asking for. But unfortunately, Eisenhower wasn't the one who determined foreign policy for the US. He let himself be pushed around by his Secretaries of State, first Dulles and now Herter" (p. 454).

The break-down of the Paris Summit ended any hopes Ike had of creating detente with the Russians. Nearly two years of preparation for the Summit was for naught. This failure became one of Ike's greatest disappointments in his presidency. Ike concentrated the efforts of his presidency on ending the Cold War, and he felt that real progress had been made. The U2 Affair thwarted all his work to create peace between the United States and the USSR. Ike communicated the following to the US allies at the Paris Conference: "I frankly admitted to the Western members of the conference that the U2 work we had carried on was both distasteful and disagreeable, but our relative intelligence position was so dangerous that I had decided there was no recourse" (Eisenhower, 1965, p. 554).

Ann Whitman, Ike's secretary, noted that since the Paris Summit, "Ike has been almost without exception in a bad humor-with me, but on the surface, he has managed to hold his temper and control emotions far better than I thought even he could" (Beschloss, 1986, p. 347). In the book *The U2 Affair*, Wise and Ross write a damning assessment of the U2 Affair and Ike as he came home from Paris. The authors claim that Eisenhower had just returned from "the most humiliating experience of his public career." The authors go on to claim, "the government of the United States had lied, admitted it lied, denied presidential responsibility, then admitted it, threatened, for all practical purposes, to continue the spy flights, then suspended them." The summit meeting had blown sky-high. The president had been publicly castigated by Khrushchev and his trip to Russia was canceled (Wise and Ross, 1960, p. 169).

Yet, in a television report to the nation when he returned, Ike was unrepentant: "The plain truth is this: when a nation needs intelligence activity, there is no time when vigilance can be relaxed. Incidentally, from Pearl Harbor, we learned that even negotiation itself can be used to conceal preparations for a surprise attack" (Baier and Whitney, 2017, p. 181). Ike was angry and felt like the Paris Summit and his expansive efforts at international arms control were a failure. At a National Security Council meeting shortly after Paris, Ike said of the U2 Affair: "All failures happen at the wrong time, and the failure of the U-2 on May first was no exception" (Devine, 1981, p. 151). Adding insult to injury, the US Congress asked Ike to explain the Paris Summit failure in a speech to a joint session of Congress. Ike could think of nothing worse, and Ike feared that this action would magnify the failure. Instead, Ike said that he would address the nation on the issue. So, on May 25, 1960, Ike sat down in front of the cameras in the Oval Office and addressed the nation.

Ike told the American people that he had gone to the Paris Summit with the hope that there would be some progress with the Soviets. Ike communicated that throughout his presidency, his greatest fear was a surprise attack on America. Therefore, he concluded the clandestine intelligence gathering by the U2 spy plane, although objectionable, was necessary for the protection of the United States. So why the false cover story, Ike rhetorically asked. Ike told all of America that the false story was "To protect the pilot, his mission, and/or intelligence processes at the time when the true facts were still undetermined." The false initial story, Ike said in a dissembling statement, had been based on "assumptions that were later proven incorrect."

Don't bluff, but don't tell everything either (Beschloss, 1986, p. 348).

Figure 24: Trial of US Pilot Gary Powers.

Ike went on to tell the American people that he offered (Khrushchev) to "discuss the matter with him in a personal meeting." But Khrushchev refused. Ike told the American people that the Soviets had long known about the U2 flights, but the flights had not been brought up by the Soviets until they did so at the Paris Summit, "Torpedoing the Conference." Although Ike was disappointed about the Summit, if he had to do it over, he would have still approved the flights if it meant, as it did according to Ike, that the flights would bring information that helped keep Americans safe. "In a nuclear war, there can be no victors-only losers. Even despots understand this. Despite the hostility of the men in the Kremlin, I remain convinced that the basic longings of the Soviet people are much like our own". The next day Ike famously said to his Cabinet that perhaps the lesson of the U2 Affair was to "count to ten before you say anything at all" (Beschloss, p. 348).

In a conversation later with Henry Cabot Lodge, US Ambassador to the United Nations, Ike admitted that the U2 flights, although of critical importance to the national security of the United States, were "illegal and, in fact, immoral" (Beschloss, 1986, p. 352).

Even after the investigations into the U2 Affair were completed in Congress, the episode was ongoing because the pilot, Gary Powers, was still being held prisoner in the Soviet Union. His trial began at the Kremlin in the Hall of Columns on August 17, 1960. It was a trial for his life, and it was his thirty-first birthday. The trial was an international spectacle. During the trial, Powers apologized for his illegal entry into Soviet airspace. Powers made it clear that he had nothing against the Soviet people, and he was doing his mission - without intent to hurt anyone. Back home at a press conference, Ike said of Powers and the trial that it "doesn't show evidence that he was brainwashed" (Beschloss, 1986, p. 372).

Powers was conflicted in his remorse and stated, "Now that I know some of the consequences of my flight, though I don't know all of them by any means...I am profoundly sorry that I had any part in it." When Powers was asked by the Soviet judge whether he had done his country a good or bad service he replied, "I would say a very bad service." Finally, the judge asked Powers if he regretted making the flight. "Yes, very much," Powers replied. Powers was finally sentenced to ten years of confinement, with the first three years of confinement served in prison. Powers and his family had feared that his sentence might be death, so ten years was some consolation. The Soviets referred to the leniency of their sentence on Powers as "socialist humaneness." Powers was told by his captors that the ten-year sentence could be reduced to 6 years with good behavior. In his book, *Bridge of Spies*, Giles Whittell contends that Powers realized that his main value to his captors was that of propaganda, and acted accordingly (Whittell, 2010, p. 183).

Back home, the American people were mixed in their reactions. Some thought "he served his country badly" at the trial. Few expected him as the hero-martyr, but many were perplexed by his admissions of guilt and contrition for performing his duty as a trained officer. Some Americans wondered if Powers was more of a mercenary than a patriot. Powers was in Soviet captivity for 1 year, 9 months, and ten days. Powers was released as part of the famous USSR/US prisoner swap that took place on February 10, 1962, at the Glienicke Bridge in Berlin. Powers and one other American were exchanged for a US-held Soviet KGB Colonel named Rudolf Abel. (Dramatized in the film with Tom Hanks called *Bridge of Spies*.) After returning to the United States, on March 2, 1962, Powers was questioned before a US Senate Armed Services Select Committee and was commended by the senators as having done his job as an officer. "There is one thing that I always remembered while I was there and that was that I am an American," said Powers (US Senate, 1962, p. 17).

In their 1962 book *The U2 Affair*, which investigated the May 1, 1960, U2 downing in the USSR, Wise and Ross hold forth that Ike and his administration made fatal missteps before, during, and after the U2 plane was shot down. "By lying, when it could have remained silent, by admitting it had lied, by disclaiming presidential responsibility, then admitting presidential responsibility, and finally by implying the flights would continue, the United States all but made it impossible for the summit meeting to take place" (Wise and Ross, 1960, p 261).

Wise and Ross contend that Ike suspected from the start that Khrushchev made such a public display of the May 1, 1960 flight, specifically so that the U2 flights would be discontinued, and then the USSR would be done with humiliation from them. Regardless, the whole fiasco contributed greatly to continued tensions between the United States and the USSR. Ike left office after eight years unable to reach detente with the USSR. Ike states in memoirs, "The big error we made was, of course, in the issuance of a premature and erroneous cover story. Allowing myself to be persuaded on this score is my principle personal regret - except for the U2 failure itself - regarding the whole affair" (Eisenhower, 1965, p. 558). Yet Ike also stated: "Regarding the U2 program itself, I know of no decision that I would make differently, given the same set of facts as they confronted us at the time" (Eisenhower, 1965, p. 558). Ike states the final words on the U2 Affair: "When I have been questioned about the wisdom of the U2 flights, I have replied with a question of my own: 'Would you be ready to give back all of the information we secured from our U2 flights over Russia if there had been no disaster to one of our planes in Russia?' I have never received an affirmative response" (Eisenhower, 1965, p. 559).

Relations between the United States and the USSR did deteriorate. In June 1960, at a Kremlin press conference, Khrushchev said that Eisenhower was "completely lacking in willpower" in his ability to stand up to the "Cold Warriors" in his administration. Khrushchev insulted Ike even more: "I think that when the President is no longer in office, we could give him a job as kindergarten director. I am sure he would not hurt the children. But it is dangerous for a man like that to run a nation...I say this because I know him" (Beschloss, 1986, p. 366). In his final verdict on the U2 Affair, Khrushchev stated: "We showed the whole world that while other Western powers might crawl on their bellies in front of America's mighty financial and industrial capital, we won't bow down-not for one second. Our goal was peace

In Good Faith

and friendship, but we wouldn't let ourselves be abused and degraded." As distorted as this statement from Khrushchev may sound, there is some truth to it (Beschloss, 1986, p. 429).

Years later, just before his death, Khrushchev indicated that the U2 Affair was the beginning of the end for his power in the USSR. The hardliners within the Kremlin began their ascent, and Khrushchev, as a seeker of detente with the US, was sidelined in favor of those who believed that the way to deal with the United States was "only military force." Khrushchev became vilified as a leader by the Politburo, and when he died his body was buried in a cemetery in Moscow, rather than the Kremlin. The main Soviet newspaper, Pravda, announced Khrushchev's death with one sentence on a back page.

Ike understood that although there were greater overarching goals between the United States and the USSR of reducing or eliminating nuclear testing and reducing nuclear arsenals, there was another more subtle goal on Ike's part. That was the goal to have better and clearer channels of communication. Direct communication could prevent an accidental nuclear conflict that could arise from misperceptions and lack of communication. Later after the 1961 failed Bay of Pigs US invasion of Cuba, Ike stated about the U2 Affair: "Considering all the information we got out of the many U-2 flights, what happens at Paris fades into insignificance. But here we gained nothing, and it made us look childish and ridiculous" (Beschloss, 1986, p. 436). In *Waging Peace*, Ike had an equally pessimistic view of the Paris Summit: "I think the Paris Summit, had it been held, would have proved to be a failure and thus would have brought the Free World only further disillusionment. Khrushchev could have used the failure as an excuse for revoking the invitation for me to visit Moscow. The U-2 incident made this easier" (Eisenhower, 1965, p. 558).

Ike did recognize that one of the most important aspects of his presidency had been to hold the line on dramatically increasing US military spending and thereby prevent further escalation of the international arms race. The downing of the U2 was one plane downed in Soviet airspace after four years of success. Shortly before he died on March 28, 1969, at 78 years of age, Ike poignantly told a friend: "I had longed to give the United States and the world a lasting peace, I was only able to contribute to a stalemate" (Beschloss, 1986, p. 437). Ike believed his inability to gain greater detente between the United States and the USSR was the single greatest failure of his presidency. In retrospect, the U2 Affair may have been the single greatest contributing event to that failure. Ike understood very well that the U2 flights were illegal and possibly even an act of war on the part of the United States. However, Ike still approved the flights. The exceptional intelligence that was gathered from the U2 flights may have prevented a war. The intelligence gathered by the U2 flights certainly prevented greater US military build-up, at least during the Eisenhower presidency.

As a man experienced with war, Ike had the keen sense that he was a man of peace in the White House. Ike understood, better than most, the existential danger that the nuclear arms race presented to humanity. Khrushchev communicated to his people, after he visited the United States, that Ike "sincerely wanted to liquidate the cold war and to improve relations." The U2 flights provided conclusive proof that the Soviets had failed to develop an ICBM through 1957. William I. Hitchcock, in his 2018 book *The Age of Eisenhower, America and the World in the 1950s*, claims that the U2 program "was the greatest American achievement since the cracking of the Japanese codes on the eve of the battle of Midway in 1942" (p. 457).

The Soviet downing of the United States U2 spy plane and the subsequent public relations fiasco for the Eisenhower administration contributed to some loss of credibility for Vice-President Nixon and his bid to win the US White House in 1960. The missile manufacturers benefited greatly from Ike's departure from the White House. US nuclear missile production increased dramatically after Ike left office. Convair, Douglas, Lockheed, and Martin Corporation saw their stock price and profits increase at a phenomenal rate as the nuclear arms race escalated. In just five years, after Ike left office, US nuclear warheads doubled from 15,000 in 1959 to 30,000 in 1964. So, there were certainly some who benefited from this lack of detente. Democratic presidential candidate, John F. Kennedy, used a ruse of the United States having a *missile gap* to help get himself elected president in 1960.

Ike's willingness to finally take the blame for the U2 Affair did demonstrate courage and honesty. A leader of a different caliber may have taken an easier way out. In his book *The Age of Eisenhower, America and the World in the 1950s*, William Hitchcock asserts that Ike's decision to claim the blame for the U2 flights may have made his staff happy, but "destroyed the Paris summit" (Hitchcock, 2018).

The famous journalist Walter Lippman claimed that Ike's willingness to take the blame, even considering that he was told by Dulles and Bissell that the U2 plane would self-destruct and that more flights should take place before the Paris Summit, was "a fatal mistake." Ike's acceptance of blame may have worsened the cold war. Maybe Ike played the wrong hand. Ike could have cast blame publicly on subordinates and maybe saved the Paris Summit and lessened the Cold War and even reversed the arms race.

Ike was a cagey, canny, and principled negotiator. Ike may have admitted wrong because he mistakenly thought his honesty would give him some stature in the negotiations. Or Ike may have misjudged the situation and sought to have his own reputation untarnished because of personal pride. All this at the expense of a major international negotiation. Ike may have sought to clear the air before the Paris negotiations in the hope that the parties could negotiate in good faith.

Although Ike took responsibility for the U2 flight, he refused to take any responsibility for the failure of the Paris Peace Summit. Ike said that the United States did nothing to justify the scorn that Khrushchev heaped upon the United States. But the failure of the Summit did dramatically reduce the chances of peace between the two nations. Indeed, the enmity increased, and the nuclear arms race escalated for decades. In his book, *The Age of Eisenhower, America, and the World in the 1950s*, William Hitchcock makes an overwhelming assertion about Ike and the U2 incident claiming that Ike's decision to approve the U2 overflights in the spring of 1960 was "the biggest mistake he ever made" (2018, p. 469).

Later in May of 1960, US Senator William Fulbright, the Democratic Party chairman of the US Senate Foreign Relations Committee, opened a Senate inquiry into the U2 events and the Paris Summit. Unsurprisingly, the Senate Committee concluded that given the upcoming Paris Summit, the U2 flights should have been canceled (Hitchcock, 2018). Senator Fulbright, as political as he was in the affair, made a harsh but insightful judgment on Ike's actions when Fulbright claimed that Ike was wrong to take the blame for the U2 downing in such a self-righteous way.

Fulbright went on in his criticism of Ike: "It is unprecedented among civilized nations for a chief of state to assume personal responsibility for covert intelligence operations." Fulbright noted that Ike pretty much forced Khrushchev to demand a personal apology from Ike (Hitchcock, 2018, p. 471).

The 43-year-old senator from Massachusetts, John F. Kennedy, (who was also by this time the 1960 presumptive Democratic presidential nominee) further attacked Ike by stating in a speech to the US Senate on June 14, 1960, that Ike's actions in the U2 affair reflected "...the illusion that good intentions and pious principles are a substitute for strong creative leadership" (Hitchcock, 2018, p. 472). Ike was attacked by the left for being pious and naive in his dealings with the Soviets and he was attacked from the right by the archconservative (and 1964 Republican Party presidential nominee) Senator Barry Goldwater. Senator Goldwater accused Ike of a massive failure in US international leadership. Ike, according to Senator Goldwater, squandered the dominant position that the United States had in the world after defeating the Nazis in WWII. Senator Goldwater, and many other US hardline conservatives, believed that Ike was failing to win the Cold War.

It is now widely viewed that Khrushchev did sincerely desire peace with the United States and did have to fight off his right flank at home - some members of the Soviet Politburo and the Soviet military - in order to pursue peace with the United States. Even later in life, Khrushchev was convinced that greater progress could have been made in US-Soviet relations if Ike had dissociated himself from the U2 Affair. Khrushchev writes in his memoirs: "As long as President Eisenhower was dissociated from the U-2 affair, we could continue our policy of strengthening Soviet-US relations which had begun with my trip to America and my talks with Eisenhower" (Khrushchev, 1974, p. 447). Khrushchev goes on to say (after Ike had personally taken responsibility for the U2 flights and further stated that the United States had a right to gather this intelligence to protect itself): "It was no longer possible for us to spare the President. He had, so to speak, offered his back end, and we obliged him by kicking it as hard as we could. Our resolute response had no immediate effect" (Khrushchev, 1974, p. 448). Khrushchev goes on to boast "The U-2 affair was a landmark event in our struggle against the American imperialists who were waging the Cold War."

A key element in all negotiations is information. Intelligence gathering as part of a negotiation is vital. The more accurate information you can have about your counterpart the better. There is almost always incomplete information in all human affairs - it is just the nature of knowledge that it is impossible to know all contingencies in all circumstances. As previously noted, the Buddhists call this phenomenon dependent origination. All events/circumstances have innumerable conditions which have given rise to those events or circumstances. It is simply impossible to know all these conditions, to have a complete picture with which to 100% accurately assess current conditions, and to make a completely informed decision. Therefore, in any given negotiation, the party which can amass more pertinent information has the strategic advantage. In the poker game of Texas Hold'em, players want the "late position" in the deal because in that position you have more knowledge - from the players that have played before you. More relevant information to a negotiator gives that negotiator greater power in the negotiation.

Also, generally in negotiation, you want your opponent to make the first move. This tips your opponent's hand in the

In Good Faith

negotiation and gives you more information with which to bargain. Ike and the US government made a mistake by tipping their hand in making the first moves to define (deceptively) what the U2 plane was doing. These missteps on the part of the United States, gave the USSR an advantage in the negotiation because they had more information - knowing that the U2 was a spy plane, and that Powers was alive.

On the other hand, through the hundreds of flights of the U2, Ike had gathered enough information to know conclusively that the missile/bomber gap between the United States and the USSR was fiction. The United States was far ahead of the USSR in missile development. In point of fact, the United States was far ahead of the USSR in missile and bomber deployment. John F. Kennedy (JFK) was inaugurated on January 20, 1961, and on January 25, 1961 JFK announced, "Flights of American aircraft penetrating the air space of the Soviet Union have been suspended since May 1960. I have ordered that they not be resumed" (Beschloss, 1986, p. 327). Khrushchev and JFK met in Vienna, Austria on the 3rd and 4th of June 1961. At this meeting, Khrushchev returned to his magnanimous self by once again stating that he knew Ike was unaware of the U2 flights, and that he had very much wanted Ike to visit the USSR. Khrushchev stated it would now be possible for an American president to visit the USSR and that JFK would be welcome at any time.

Sometimes negotiation lacks a middle way. In the case of the U2 Affair and the broader Cold War, Ike's middle way failed to increase world peace. Negotiation failed. Strong sides of a negotiation can have mutually exclusive interests. In the case of the U2 Affair, the two sides failed to compromise. The stalemate of the Cold War along with the

179

unconscionable build-up of nuclear weapons between the United States and the USSR ensued for decades.

Chapter 7
Eisenhower and the Middle Way of Strong Negotiation.

In his 1987 book *The Eisenhower Presidency,* Kenneth W. Thompson refers to Ike as a *Principled Pragmatist.* So the call is to practice Principled Pragmatism in your negotiations. Work from a set of Principles (Thompson, 1987, p. 16). "All leadership - political, economic, or moral - involves persuading others to do something now that will bring fruit in the future" (DDE, 27 August 1958).

Strong Negotiation is the *Middle Way.* Too often Strong Negotiation is associated with forceful, aggressive, or hard-driven bargaining. True strong negotiation is flexible, calmly persistent, and patient, rather than hard-charging, position-taking, and uncompromising. The middle way in negotiating sounds like it is the easiest, but it is, in fact, the most difficult and usually the most time-consuming route in negotiating. Taking the soft way out in negotiating is failing to accept the responsibility of the job. Taking the hard way in negotiating is also being lazy in the job because this position usually fails to recognize the legitimate concerns of your counterpart. Imagine a pushy car salesperson who just wants to sell you the car on the lot, rather than listening to you about the car you want to buy. As Ike points out in the middle way, "All human experience tends to show that human progress, where advanced numbers of people and intricate relationships are concerned, is possible only as extremes are avoided and solutions to problems are found in a great middle way that has regard for the requirements, desires, and aspirations of the vast majority" (Eisenhower, 1996, p. 359).

In an anonymously published essay in 1922 in the magazine, *Infantry Journal,* after Ike had left his military graduate training at Leavenworth, Ike had this advice for future graduate students: "Use common sense; don't magnify the importance of insignificant details; don't worry about bygones; and keep it simple" (Smith, 2012, p. 73).

In a family setting, for example, the middle way might be expressed as follows: Let us say that there is a dispute between two parents on how to discipline their child after misbehavior. One parent recommends that the discipline should be very harsh, the other parent states that discipline is unnecessary given the nature of the offense. The harsh discipline parent insists on the harsh discipline and states that the discussion is done. The no discipline parent concedes to the harsher discipline parent without much conversation. Here, both parents have abdicated their responsibility as advocates for and negotiators on behalf of the health of their child. The lenient parent has taken the soft way of negotiation, and the harsh parent has taken the hard way of negotiation.

The middle way of this negotiation would be the most difficult and the longest way of negotiation whereby each parent would carefully listen to the other; together they would deliberate on the consequences of the misbehavior for their child - coming to a compromise on the agreed-upon consequences for their child. Neither parent would get the exact discipline they want for their child. This is an example of a negotiation where both parties want the best for their child. Yet, many negotiations lack such apparent common interests and shared goals.

In the Suez Crisis, the French and the British intended to continue to exert colonial control over the Egyptians and the Suez Canal. This position was untenable in the negotiations

– and the British and the French were coerced by the United States and the United Nations into accepting a compromise. Ike took the middle way between military force and inaction. The successful negotiations to end the Suez Crisis involved the carrot and the stick. The carrot for Nasser was that the Suez Canal would remain in Egypt's control - with some oversight. The stick part was how Ike coerced the leaders of France, England, and Israel to cease and desist from their invasion of Egypt.

Ike communicated to the UK and France (among other things) that they would soon have a serious problem getting oil to their countries, and that reserves of the French franc and the British pound would suffer. Ike communicated to Israel that Israel would suffer severe economic sanctions should Israel refuse to remove forces from Egypt. In addition to the US opposition to the violation of the rule of law, (France and the UK had violated Article 1 of the NATO pact), Ike also saw it as an opportunity to increase the US influence in the Middle East. This was a strategy to prevent additional influence by the USSR in the Middle East.

The single greatest driving force in the Eisenhower administration in favor of the 1957 Civil Rights Act was the US Attorney General, Herbert Brownell. Brownell stepped down as US Attorney General shortly after the Act was signed into law in September of 1957. In the culmination of the Civil Rights Act of 1957, the Southern Segregationists refused any repudiation of Southern segregation, aka their *way of life*. The segregationists were forced into accepting some protections on the right of African Americans to vote. The segregationists refused to accept the CRA of 1957 or any other Voting Rights Act. (A law passed by the US Congress, upheld by the US Supreme Court, and enforced by the US Executive Branch.) Ike took the middle way.

The final vote in the US House was 285-126, Republicans 167-19, and Democrats 118-117. But it was the US Senate where the real negotiations took place. In the US Senate, the vote on the Act was 72-18, with Republicans voting 43-0 in favor, while Democrats voted 29-18 in favor. DDE successfully used the ambition and the skill of LBJ to get the Act passed into law. Ike knew that LBJ, a Southerner, and a masterful leader of the US Senate, was much better equipped than he was to bring the 1957 CRA across the finish line.

Ike had some connections to the decisions that led to the deployment of US troops to Korea. Ike was appointed Supreme Commander Europe shortly after the North Koreans invaded South Korea on June 25, 1950. In 1950, President Truman appointed General Douglas MacArthur Chief of the United Nations Command (UNC) for Korea upon the unanimous recommendation of the US Joint Chiefs of Staff. In April of 1951, President Truman relieved General MacArthur of his command for insubordination. Truman's famous quote sums it all up pretty well: "I fired him because he wouldn't respect the authority of the President…I didn't fire him because he was a dumb son of a bitch, although he was, but that's not against the law for generals. If it was, half to three-quarters of them would be in jail" (Miller, 2018, p. 308).

By the 1952 presidential election between Adlai Stevenson and DDE, tens of thousands of US lives had been lost in Korea, along with millions of Chinese and Korean civilians and combatants. The American, Chinese, and Korean people were all weary of the conflict. Ike campaigned in 1952 on ending the Korean War, and he did end the War. As soon as Ike was elected, he traveled to Korea and assessed the situation. Upon his return to the United States, Ike quickly directed his staff to begin final negotiations for an Armistice,

In Good Faith

which took place at a fast pace, within 6-8 months, in July of 1953.

The South Koreans, the North Koreans, the Chinese, the United Nations, and the United States all accepted the Korean Armistice because a ceasefire and end of violence were in their individual interest. The fighting ended - without winners or losers. There was a compromise, but a compromise that ultimately contributed to the ongoing murderous oppression of the North Korean people.

Ike was truly an *honest broker* and a catalyst for a settlement in the Steel Strike of 1959. Ike had the best interests of the American people in mind as he sought a solution to this strike, which lasted 116 days from 15 July 1959 to 7 November 1959. Approximately 500,000 US steelworkers went on strike, which affected a substantial part of the US economy. Ike sought numerous times to bring the parties together for a negotiated settlement. However, management and labor were very dug-in, selfish, and hostile to one another. Ike did invoke the Taft-Hartley Act to force the workers back on the job, but this was temporary. A compromise, which favored labor, was finally brokered. But it was a pyrrhic victory for the USWA as the US steel industry and thus the USWA began a long dramatic decline.

In the US Steel Strike of 1959, the Steelworkers Union won the battle but lost the war. The narrow and hard interests of both labor and management in the Steel Strike cost the US economy greatly in 1959 and on into the future. In 1959, the USWA was the most powerful union in the United States. Ike took the middle way between labor and management to find a compromise that both sides could finally live with.

Ike had few choices when it came to the aftermath of the U2 incident. The U2 pilot Francis Gary Powers was captured, tried by the Supreme Soviet, and convicted of espionage. The USSR held Powers for almost two years. Ike did not negotiate his way out of the U2 incident. Ultimately, Ike told the truth about the U2 plane, and he let the negotiations play out. Khrushchev sabotaged the Paris Peace Summit in May 1960, and Ike's hope of a lasting legacy of arms control vanished. Ike salvaged very little from the incident, and the US/USSR relations deteriorated further into the Cold War.

Several Eisenhower historians consider the U2 Affair the worst event in Ike's tenure as a US president. Ike took it in stride, but he was angry and remorseful, nonetheless. Ike misjudged the circumstances. Ike took a calculated risk for several years with the U2 flights. Some question if intelligence gathered by the U2 program may not have been worth a loss of detente with the USSR.

In the U2 incident, the Soviets got the spectacle they wanted, and President Eisenhower upheld his integrity. The May 1960 Paris Peace talks between the United States, the USSR, Great Britain, and France were a fiasco, in large part because of the U2 incident. It is unclear whether any arms control agreements would have come from the 1960 Peace talks, but the U2 incident took that possibility off the table. Ike sought disarmament with the Soviet Union through some compromise. Ike failed to produce detente with the Soviet Union. In addition, President John F. Kennedy rapidly increased the US nuclear stockpile, and all but eliminated any arms control agreements until many years later.

Ike was one of the most articulate and well-written of all the US presidents. Ike practiced his entire life to be an effective communicator. His daily discipline of writing included his diaries, correspondence, and policy commentary and analysis. As a military commander, Ike wrote extensively each day - and he practiced writing concisely and with

In Good Faith

precision - communicating clearly to superiors, subordinates, the troops, the public, and the press.

Ike was a thorough and generally concise communicator. In working with various speechwriters and staff throughout his career, Ike was fond of asking QED? QED is an acronym for the Latin phrase *quod erat demonstrandum*. This phrase is translated, "what has to be demonstrated." In other words, it means roughly what's the point? What is the bottom line? Ike's White House speechwriter, Fred Fox, summed it up, "The General believes that if you can't put your bottom-line message on the back of a matchbook before you begin typing, you're wasting his time and yours" (Humes, 2001, p. 245). Ike could also dissemble successfully, playing the absent-minded old man, or the fool to "catch the wise" with the press. Another Latin phrase that Ike liked was *Acta Non Verba*, which is translated as "Actions, not words" (Humes, 2001, p. 244).

The ability to persuade engenders power, and with power also comes the ability to persuade. According to Ike's colleagues, Ike had a simple definition of power "the ability to produce a desired result." In negotiation, the power of persuasion has many elements: charm, wit, patience, persistence, empathy, and listening. Persuasion can employ coercion. Personal integrity is also persuasive.

Military power as a form of persuasion is only one part of the ability to produce a desired result. Ike was a believer in extreme restraint in the use of force. Ike cautioned that in international affairs, a leader "should never use force. But if you do use it, use it overwhelmingly" (Thompson, 1987, p. 22). In the realm of international affairs and negotiation, Ike believed in the power of consensus and of the power of public support. Ike understood that without the consent of the governed, power was illegitimate and unsustainable in its use. Ike worked throughout his presidency to maintain the consensus and the trust of the American people.

Individual and collective negotiating power also comes directly from collective and individual freedom. As Ike said in his famous speech before he became a US president, to the American Bar Association, which outlined his political and personal philosophy in St. Louis, Missouri, September 5,1949: "First, that individual freedom is our most precious possession. It is to be guarded as the chief heritage of our people, the wellspring of our spiritual and material greatness, and the central target of all enemies - internal and external - who seek to weaken or destroy the American Republic" (Medhurst, 1993, p. 134). Ike went on in the same speech to describe how the *middle of the road* of America is the source of its great power: "The middle of the road is derided by all of the right and of the left. They deliberately misrepresent the central position as a neutral, wishy-washy one. Yet here is the truly creative area in which we may obtain agreement for constructive social action compatible with basic American principles and with the just aspirations of every sincere American. It is the area in which is rooted in the hopes and allegiance of the vast majority of people" (Medhurst, 1993, p. 136).

According to the political scientist and historian Kenneth W. Thompson in his essay entitled "The Strengths and Weaknesses of Eisenhower's Leadership," Ike knew that power could be a "mix of military, political, and psychological factors." Ike also knew that the power of public opinion and overall morale was necessary to good policy (Thompson, 1987, p. 25). Strong negotiation is negotiating from a position of strength of principle, consensus, and integrity. True strength comes from consensus. Always negotiate from a position of power -

power as integrity of purpose, and power as action in good faith.

Ike had a strong and abiding religious faith throughout his life. Both of his parents were devout Christians, as they were members of the River Brethren Church in Abilene, Kansas. The River Brethren Church was an offshoot of the Mennonite faith. From a young age, Ike's life was formed around work and faith. The Eisenhower children studied Scripture each morning and each evening. Ike could cite by rote, long passages of the Bible, and often integrated Biblical wisdom into his writing and speaking. As the authors, Sears, Osten, and Cole put it in their book about Ike's faith entitled *The Soul of An American President*, "Ike clearly lived with the Christian paradox that people must constantly strive to live with virtue while acknowledging in faith that all of our efforts are useless without God's grace" (2019, p. 99).

As a point of fact, in his domestic and international policies, Ike often had more support from moderate Democrats and moderate Republicans in the US Congress and US Governorships than he did from right-wing Republicans and left-wing Democrats. Ike is sometimes credited with saving the Republican Party from its isolationist wing. Senator Robert Taft of Ohio represented this isolationist wing of the Republican party and was Ike's chief Republican Party rival (Ike initially lost the nomination to Taft at the 1952 Republican Convention in Chicago) for the US presidential nomination in 1952. Taft led a group called the America First Committee. Isolationist conservatives such as Taft preached US international isolationism, trade protectionism, and small government.

According to the Eisenhower biographer, Jean Edward Smith: "As a military statesman, Ike's emphasis on team play, his willingness to compromise, and his ability to reconcile diverse interests were unique assets" (Smith, 2012, p. 194). Ike understood the necessity of planning: "Plans are worthless, but planning is everything." In negotiations, as in life, "Fortune favors the prepared mind." The possession of worthwhile information usually provides the holder with an edge in negotiation. Find out your opponent's weaknesses. What does your opponent want? Why is your counterpart negotiating with you? Does your opponent have secrets? What are the courses of action that your counterpart has? Be prepared.

For the most part, Ike surrounded himself with many competent, even brilliant, individuals. Ike depended heavily on technical and scientific advisers. Ike also depended greatly on close friends, family, and confidants. He once said to an advisor, "Just because I accept your advice, does not mean I have to like it." Ike relied on input to devise a strategy, examine options, and think out loud. Herbert Brownell, Ike's US Attorney General from 1953-1957, had this to say about Ike's approach to his staff: "I have said that in my judgment he was the best practitioner of consultative management that I have ever seen in operation in the public sector or the private sector" (Thompson, 1984, p. 233).

Ike said that he saw his leadership (negotiation) as "largely in making progress through compromise" (Crockett, 2002, p. 134). Ike sought consensus in most of his decisions. Yet Ike "also had a reputation for not intervening in the work of others, and letting others take credit and take blame" (Devine, 1981, p. 135). Ike's public leadership sometimes seemed reluctant. Ike sometimes failed to use moral leadership in some areas where he had the public support to do so, such as desegregation of schools.

Patience in negotiation keeps time on your side. Whoever is most impatient in negotiations has the biggest disadvantage.

Ike generally took time on important decisions that required greater deliberation: "Unless circumstances and responsibility demanded an instant judgment, I learned to reserve mine until the last proper moment" (Kowert, 2002, p. 34).

The historian Steven Ambrose adds, "In retrospect, what stands out about Eisenhower's crisis management is that at every stage, he kept his options open. Flexibility was one of his chief characteristics as Supreme Commander in World War II. He never knew himself just how he would respond to an invasion of Quemoy and Matsu because he insisted on waiting to see the precise nature of the attack before deciding how to react" (1990, p. 385).

Ike did his best to demonstrate emotional control, and he knew that it was dangerous to condemn or belittle a person. "A man will respect you and perhaps even like you if you differ with him on issues and principles. But if you ever challenge his motives, he will never forgive you. Nor should he" (Polsky, 2015, p. 17).

It is worth noting, that in all his eight years as president, and his three or four decades as a military commander, no one left working with Ike and then wrote a 'tell-all' book that execrated Ike (Thompson, 1987, p. 15). Ike has this to say about the ethics of leadership and negotiation: "I think it is fair to say that, in this situation, only a leadership that is based on honesty of purpose, calmness, an inexhaustible patience in conference and persuasion, and refusal to be diverted from basic principles can, in the long run, win out" (Eisenhower, 1963, p. 193).

Ike goes on to describe the essential qualities of ethical leadership and negotiation: "Clearly, there are different ways to try to be a leader. In my view, a fair, decent, and reasonable dealing with men, a reasonable recognition that views may diverge, a constant seeking for a high and strong ground on which to work together, is of us. A living democracy needs diversity to keep it strong. For survival, it also needs to have the diversities brought together in a common purpose, so fair, so reasonable, and so appealing that all can rally to it" (Eisenhower, p. 193).

Ike understood the necessity of taking time to make better decisions when you have the opportunity to do so: "Boy, there's just one thing I really *know*. You *can't* decide things in *panic*. Any decision you make when you are panicked, you can be sure of only one thing. It will be a bad one" (Hughes, 1963, p. 252).

Historian Stephen Ambrose points out that Ike spent a great deal of his time negotiating with Allied Leaders in WWII, and once he became the 34th US President "Eisenhower had spent his life working out compromises between strong-willed people" (2014, p. 29). "Indeed, I argued that in great human affairs the middle-of-the-road approach was the only one that provided any avenue for progress and the extremists both of reaction and so-called liberalism should be abjured like the plague" (Galambos, Daun Van Ee, 2001, pg. 1752).

According to the historian Paul A. Kowert in his book *Groupthink or Deadlock: When Do Leaders Learn from Their Advisors,* Ike dealt with dissent. "He was able to manage conflict among his associates and to learn from it" (2002, p. 38). One of Ike's closest associates, and Ike's WWII Chief of Staff, General Walter Bedell Smith, had this to say about Ike's decision-making style: "He had great patience, and he disdains no advice regardless of source. One of his most successful methods in dealing with individuals is to assume he himself is lacking in detailed knowledge and liable to make an error and is seeking advice. This is by no means a pose, because he actually values the recommendations and suggestions he receives" (Kowert, 2002, pp. 39-40).

Ike knew that as president, many of the most consequential decisions came down to him. Ike liked to tell the story of President Abraham Lincoln: "On a crucial question during the Civil War, Abraham Lincoln is said to have called for a vote around the Cabinet Table. Every member voted no. 'The ayes have it,' Lincoln announced. The presidency still works the same way today" (Kowert, 2002, p. 46).

Ike sometimes advocated the non-consensus path. Ike shunned the Congressional approach of horse-trading, which Ike believed often resulted in modifying and placating. "They (congresspersons) do not seem to realize when there arrives that moment at which soft speaking should be abandoned, and a fight to the end undertaken. Any man who hopes to exercise leadership must be ready to meet this requirement face to face when it arises; unless he is ready to fight when necessary, people will finally begin to ignore him" (Polsky, 2015, p. 20). "We hold it to be the first task of statesmanship to develop the strength that will deter the forces of aggression and promote the conditions of peace" (Eisenhower, Inaugural Address, 1953).

In Review, Pictures I've Kept, 1969, published the year Ike died, Ike had this to say about leadership: "A human understanding and a natural ability to mingle with all men on a basis of equality are more important than any degree of technical skill" (Eisenhower, p. 59).

Ike and his associates had the technical skills, but more importantly, Ike came from humble origins and could "mingle with all men," while he negotiated "In Good Faith."

Lou Villaire

Afterward

Figure 25: Ike Signing 1957 Civil Rights Act.

In the preceding pages, five historical events occurred during the eight years of the Eisenhower presidency. In these crises, The Korean War, The Suez Invasion, the US civil rights movement, the 1959 Steel Strike, and the U2 Affair, Ike is seen at his best and his worst. The lessons of history from these stories are practical. History is indeed our best teacher - even if we often fail to learn. Here the lessons of history are captivating and pragmatic.

Ike displays his numerous superior strategies, tactics, and skills in negotiation. He also shows his "personal equation" which includes a great understanding of human motivations

Lou Villaire

- why we do what we do. Ike shows us his weaknesses and his mistakes. It is good to think that Ike would be pleased and amused that we can learn from his actions and put those lessons to work in our own lives to be stronger negotiators.

It may sound shopworn or even dull, but what has attracted me to Dwight David Eisenhower for well over a decade now is his underappreciated *middle way* of strong negotiation. His gentle in manner (usually), strong in deed philosophy, and his unpretentious practice of life, endure as a profound message for individuals and our Nation.

Acknowledgments

Many thanks go to the staff at the Eisenhower Presidential Library who kindly assisted me in my several visits. Thank you to the many, many Eisenhower scholars who have illuminated his life and accomplishments. And thank you to my business partners and co-workers who have endured my Eisenhower obsession for many years.

This book would not have come about without faith and the support and encouragement of my family, friends, colleagues, and co-workers. Our daughter Bella endured many quiet early mornings with her father writing the book. Our son Gus asked about the book from time to time and was generous with his encouragement. Gus even helped with the design of the book cover and invested monetarily in its publication. And my deepest appreciation and greatest love go to my spouse, Joan Axthelm. Thank you, Love.

Lou Villaire

In Good Faith

Photograph Credits

Cover Photograph: Alamy Photos, alamy.com "Four Various Moods of US President Dwight Eisenhower" during a press conference, Washington, DC, USA, 1960.

Figure 1: Puryear, Jr. 1971, 1992, 289

Figure 2: 7 June 1944, English Channel, Eisenhower Library.

Figure 3: Eisenhower 1952 Republican National Convention.

Figure 4: 38th Parallel Korean War.

Figure 5: Eisenhower visit to Korea Christmas 1952.

Figure 6: Colonel-level discussions between the US and North Korean militaries on 11 October 1951, U.S. National Archives and Records Administration.

Figure 7: UN delegate Lieut. Gen. William K. Harrison, Jr. (seated left), and Korean People's Army and Chinese People's Volunteers Delegate Gen. Nam Il (seated right) signing the Korean War armistice agreement at P'anmunjŏm, Korea, July 27, 1953. U.S. Department of Defense (F. Kazukaitis. U.S. Navy).

Figure 8: Suez Troop Movement, Suez Canal 1956.

Figure 9: Suez Canal, Egypt, Circa 1956, Public Domain.

Figure 10: Eisenhower and Gamal Abdel Nasser, Cir 1956, Wikipedia Commons.

Figure 11: Troop Movements, Suez Invasion, 1956. Photo Association for Diplomatic Studies & Training, adst.org

Figure 12: Eisenhower and US Secretary of State, John Foster Dulles, 1956, Public Domain.

Figure 13: Protest for Civil Rights, 1957.

Figure 14: Eisenhower Listening in 1957 CRA Debate.

Figure 15: The Little Rock Nine Escorted to School in Arkansas by the US National Guard.

Figure 16: Senator Lyndon Johnson. US Senate Majority Leader and Georgia Senator Richard Russell, Lyndon Baines Johnson Library and Museum. Image Serial Number: W98-30 http://photolab.lbjlib.utexas.edu/detail.asp?id=14899.

Figure 17: Eisenhower with US Civil Rights Leaders, White House Albums, National Park Service (Abbie Rowe): Photographs.

Figure 18: Steel Mills at Gary in 1973, Indiana. Photo by Sequeira, Paul.

Figure 19: USWA Cleveland Local 1157 on Strike 1959.

Figure 20: Eisenhower and Press Secretary James Haggerty.

Figure 21: US U2 Spy plane, Circa 1955.

Figure 22: The Central Intelligence Agency and Overhead Reconnaissance: The U-2 and OXCART Programs, 1954-1974 173 (pdf p.186). History Staff, Central Intelligence Agency (1992).

Figure 23: Khrushchev viewing wreckage of the U2, Eisenhower Presidential Library.

Figure 24: Trial of US U2 Pilot Gary Powers, Soviet Politburo, USSR

Figure 25: Ike Signing 1957 Civil Rights Act, Eisenhower Presidential Library.

Bibliography

Adams, Sherman. 1961. *First-hand Reports: the Inside Story of the Eisenhower Administration*. New York, NY: Harper.

A&E Television Networks, LLC. n.d. "This Day in History: 11 April 1951." History.com. Accessed July 18, 2018. https://www.history.com/this-day-in-history/truman-relieves-macarthur-of-duties-in-korea.

A&E Television Networks, LLC. n.d. "This Day In History: June 27, 1950." History.com. Accessed July 25, 2019. https://www.history.com/this-day-in-history/truman-orders-u-s-forces-to-korea-2.

Ambrose, Stephen E. 1981. *Ike's Spies, Eisenhower, and the Espionage Establishment*. Jackson, MS: University Press of Mississippi.

Ambrose, Stephen E. 1990. *Eisenhower: Soldier and President*. Vol. 1. New York, NY: Simon & Schuster.

The American Presidency Project. n.d. "1956." The American Presidency Project. Accessed June 15, 2018. https://www.presidency.ucsb.edu/statistics/elections/1952.

The American Presidency Project. n.d. "1952." The American Presidency Project. Accessed June 15, 2018. https://www.presidency.ucsb.edu/statistics/elections/1952.

The American Presidency Project. 1952. "Republican Party Platform of 1952." The American Presidency Project. https://www.presidency.ucsb.edu/documents/republican-party-platform-1952.

The American Presidency Project. 1952. "1952 Democratic Party Platform." The American Presidency Project. https://www.presidency.ucsb.edu/documents/1952-democratic-party-platform.

Anderson, J. W. 1964. *Eisenhower, Brownell, and the Congress, The Tangled Origins of the Civil Rights Bill of 1956-1957*. Tuscaloosa, AL: University of Alabama Press.

Baier, Bret, and Catherine Whitney. 2017. *Three Days in January, Dwight Eisenhower's Final Mission*. New York, NY: William Morrow.

Beschloss, Michael R. 1986. *Mayday: Eisenhower, Khrushchev, and the U2 Affair*. New York, NY: Harper & Row.

Bissell, Jr., Richard M., Thomas Soapes, and Ed Edwin. 1967, 1976. *Oral History, Richard M. Bissell, Jr*. Abilene, KS: The Eisenhower Presidential Library.

Board of Inquiry. 1959. *Report To The President, The 1959 Labor Dispute In The Steel Industry*. Washington, D.C., D.C.: The Board of Inquiry Under Executive Orders 10843 and 10848.

Britannica and Michael Ray. n.d. "Korean war Timeline." Britannica.com. Accessed October 23, 2019. https://www.britannica.com/list/korean-war-timeline.

Carnegie, Dale. 2009. *How to Win Friends and Influence People*. New York, NY: Simon and Schuster.

Caro, Robert A. 2002. *The Years of Lyndon Johnson: Master of the Senate*. New York, NY: Vintage Books.

Columbia Broadcasting System, CBS. 1964. *CBS Reports: D Day Plus 20 Years - Eisenhower Returns To Normandy*. New York, New York: Columbia Broadcasting System. https://www.cbsnews.com/video/cbs-reports-1964-d-day-plus-20-years-eisenhower-returns-to-normandy/.

Crabtree, Steve. 2003. "The Gallup Brain: Americans and the Korean War." The Gallup Brain: Americans and the Korean War. https://news.gallup.com/poll/7741/gallup-brain-americans-korean-war.aspx.

Crockett, David A. 2002. *The Opposition Presidency Leadership and the Constraints of History*. College Station, TX: Texas A&M University Press.

Davis, Kenneth Sydney, *The Politics of Honor A Biography of Adlai E. Stevenson,* 1967, the University of California Press, Berkeley, CA.

Devine, Robert A. 1981. *Eisenhower and the Cold War*. New York, NY: Oxford University Press, USA.

Doran, Michael. 2016. *Ike's Gamble*. New York, NY: Free Press.

The Editors of Encyclopedia Britannica. 2012. "Paticca-samuppada." Britannica.com. https://www.britannica.com/topic/paticca-samuppada.

Edwin, Ed. 1967. *Oral History Interview with John Eisenhower*. Abilene, KS: Columbia University Oral History Project, Dwight D. Eisenhower Library.

Eisenhower, Dwight D. "Ike's Letters to a Friend," Edited with Introduction and Notes by Robert Griffith, 2021, University Press of Kansas, Lawrence, KS.

Eisenhower, David. 2010. *Going Home to Glory: A Memoir of Life with Dwight D. Eisenhower. 1961-1969*. New York, NY: Simon & Schuster.

Eisenhower, Dwight D. Containing the Public Messages, Speeches, and Statements of the President, 1953-1960/61 Volume 6, U.S. Government Printing Office, 1958, Washington, D.C.

Eisenhower, Dwight D. 1952. "I Shall Go to Korea." Eisenhower Presidential Library. https://www.eisenhowerlibrary.gov/sites/default/files/research/online-documents/korean-war/i-shall-go-to-korea-1952-10-24.pdf.

Eisenhower, Dwight D. 1952. "I Shall Go to Korea." *New York Times* (New York, Print edition), October 25, 1952. https://timesmachine.nytimes.com/timesmachine/1952/10/25/83800979.html?pageNumber=8.

Eisenhower, Dwight D. 1953. "The President's News Conference." Public Papers of the Presidents of the United States. www.federal register.gov.

Eisenhower, Dwight D. 1956. *1956 Campaign.* Abilene, KS: The White House, Eisenhower Presidential Library.

Eisenhower, Dwight D. 1957. *Letter to South Carolina Governor James F. Byrnes.* Abilene, KS: Eisenhower Presidential Library.

Eisenhower, Dwight D. 1957. *Personal Letter to Swede Hazlett.* Abilene, KS: Eisenhower Presidential Library.

Eisenhower, Dwight D. 1957. *Telephone Call Between President Eisenhower and Lyndon Johnson.* Abilene, KS: Eisenhower Presidential Library.

Eisenhower, Dwight D. 1957. *Telephone Call Transcript Between President Eisenhower and Senate Majority Leader Lyndon Johnson.* Abilene, Kansas: Eisenhower Presidential Library.

Eisenhower, Dwight D, "The Presidents's News Conference Online" by Gerhard Peters and John T. Woolley, The American Presidency Project https:www.presidency.ucsb.edu/node/233138

Eisenhower, Dwight D. 1957. *Telephone Call with US Attorney General Herbert Brownell*. Abilene, KS: Eisenhower Presidential Library.

Eisenhower, Dwight D. 1959. "Letter From the President." In *Letter from the President to the Principals in the 1959 US Steel Strike*. Washington, D.C., D.C.: The White House.

Eisenhower, Dwight D. 1959. *Memorandum For the Record*. Washington, D.C., D.C.: The White House.

Eisenhower, Dwight D. 1963. *Mandate for Change, 1953-1956*. New York, NY: Doubleday.

Eisenhower, Dwight D. 1965. *Waging Peace: 1956-1961*. New York, NY: Doubleday.

Eisenhower, Dwight D. 1967. *At Ease: Stories I Tell to Friends*. New York, NY: Doubleday.

Eisenhower, Dwight D. 1981. *The Eisenhower Diaries*. Edited by Robert H. Ferrell. New York, NY: Norton.

Eisenhower, Dwight D. 2017. "State of the Union Address: Dwight D. Eisenhower." InfoPlease. https://www.infoplease.com/primary-sources/government/presidential-speeches/state-union-address-dwight-d-eisenhower-january-10-1957.

Eisenhower, Dwight D., and Edwin Corbin. 1969. *In Review: Pictures I've Kept A Concise Pictorial Autobiography*. New York, NY: Doubleday.

Eisenhower, Dwight D., Louis Galambos, and Daun Van Ee. 2001. *The Papers of Dwight David Eisenhower*. Vol. 17. 21 vols. Baltimore, MD: Johns Hopkins University Press.

Eisenhower, Dwight D., and James C. Hagerty. 1959. *Statement by The President*. Washington, D.C., D.C.: The White House.

Eisenhower, Dwight D., and James C. Hagerty. August 2, 1957. *Statement by the President*. Washington, D.C., D.C.: White House, Press Secretary to the President.

Eisenhower, Dwight D., and James C. Hagerty. 9 October 1959. "White House Press Release." In *The White House Statement by the President*. Washington, D.C.: The White House.

Eisenhower, Dwight D., and James C. Hagerty. 19 October 1959. *Statement By The President*. Washington, D.C.: The White House.

Eisenhower, Dwight D., and David J. McDonald. 1959. "An Exchange of Letters Between the President and David J. MacDonald, President of the United Steelworkers of America." In *Letter From President Eisenhower to David J. McDonald 27 June 1959*. Washington, D.C.: The White House.

Eisenhower, John S. 2004. *General Ike: A Personal Reminiscence*. New York, NY: The Free Press.

Eisenhower, Susan. 2020. *How Ike Led: The Principles Behind Eisenhower's Biggest Decisions*. New York, NY: Thomas Dunne Books.

Ewald, Jr., William B. 1981. *Eisenhower the President: Crucial Days: 1951-1960*. Englewood Cliffs, NJ: Prentice Hall, Inc.

Fisher, Roger, and Daniel Shapiro. 2005. *Beyond Reason: Using Emotions as You Negotiate*. New York, NY: Penguin Books USA.

Fisher, Roger, and Bill Ury. 2011. *Getting to Yes: Negotiating Agreement Without Giving In*. 3RD ed. New York, NY: Penguin Books.

Goldberg, Arthur J., United Steelworkers of America, and The Board of Inquiry, Created By Executive Order. 9 October 1959. *In the Matter of the Labor Disputes Between The United Steelworkers of America and Certain Companies in the Steel Industry*. Vol. The National Emergency Issue. 1 vols. Washington, D.C.: The Board of Inquiry.

Goodpaster, Andrew J. 1960. *Memorandum For The Record*. Washington, D.C, D.C.: White House.

Graduate, A. Y. 1922. "The Leavenworth Course." *Infantry Journal* 60 (June).

Greenstein, Fred I. 1994. *The Hidden Hand Presidency: Eisenhower As leader*. 1st ed. Baltimore, MD: Johns Hopkins University Press.

Hall, Christopher G. 1979. *Steel Phoenix: The Fall and Rise of the US Steel Industry*. New York, NY: St. Martin's Press.

Hitchcock, William I. 2018. *The Age of Eisenhower, America and the World in the 1950s*. New York, NY: Simon & Schuster.

Hoover, J. E. 1956. *Racial Tension and Civil Rights*. Washington, D.C., USA: United States Department of Justice, Federal Bureau of Investigation.

Hughes, Emmet J. 1963. *The Ordeal of Power: A Political Memoir of the Eisenhower Years*. New York, NY: Atheneum.

Humes, J. C. 2001. *Eisenhower and Churchill, The Partnership That Saved The World*. Roseville, CA: Forum Press.

Hutchison, Van W. 2006. "Eisenhower Era Politics and the 1959 Steel Strike." *Madison Historical Review* 3:Article 2.

Immerman, Richard H. 1990. *John Foster Dulles: Piety, Pragmatism and Power in US Foreign Policy*. Princeton, NJ: Princeton University Press.

Khrushchev, Nikita. 1974. *Khrushchev Remembers: The Last Testament*. Translated by Strobe Talbott. Boston, MA: Little, Brown, and Company.

Khrushchev, Nikita. 2013. *Memoirs of Nikita Khrushchev: Reformer, 1945-1964*. Vol. 3. 3 vols. University Park, PA: Pennsylvania State University Press.

King, Martin Luther, *The Papers of Martin Luther King, Jr., Volume IV Symbol of Movement, January 1957-December 1958*, 1992, University of California Press, Oakland, CA.

Kissinger, Henry. 2012. *Diplomacy*. New York, NY: Simon and Schuster.

Korda, Michael. 2007. *Ike: An American Hero*. New York, NY: Harper.

Kowert, Paul A. 2002. *Groupthink or Deadlock: When Do Leaders Learn from Their Advisors?* Albany, NY: State University of New York Press.

Luter, John. 1970. *Oral History With General Mark W. Clark*. Abilene, KS: Columbia University Oral History Project at Dwight D. Eisenhower Presidential Library.

Medhurst, Martin J. 1993. *Dwight D. Eisenhower: Strategic Communicator*. Westport, CT: Greenwood Press.

Mieczkowski, Yanek. 2013. *Eisenhower's Sputnik Moment, The Race for Space and World Prestige*. Ithaca, NY: Cornell University Press.

Miller, Merle, *"Plain Speaking: An Oral Biography of Harry S. Truman,* 2018 Rosetta Books, NY, NY.

Mitchell, James P. 1959. "The Steel Strike of 1959." In *Letter to President Eisenhower*, 1. Washington, D.C.: The White House.

Morgan, Gerald D. August 15, 1957. *Memorandum For The President, Subject: Compromise Civil Rights Proposal.* Washington, D.C., D.C.: The White House.

Nathan, James A, and Oliver, James K, *United States Foreign Policy and World Order,* 1985, Little Brown Publishers, NY, NY.

National Archives. 2016. "US Enters the Korean Conflict." National Archives: Educator Resources. https://www.archives.gov/education/lessons/korean-conflict.

Nichols, David A. 2007. *A Matter of Justice: Eisenhower and the Beginning of the Civil Rights Revolution.* New York, NY: Simon & Schuster.

Nichols, David A. 2011. *Eisenhower 1956 The President's Year of Crisis--Suez and the Brink of War.* New York, NY: Simon & Schuster.

Pach, Jr., Chester J. n.d. "DWIGHT D. EISENHOWER: CAMPAIGNS AND ELECTIONS." Millercenter.org. Accessed 6 15, 2019. https://millercenter.org/president/eisenhower/campaigns-and-elections.

Polsky, Andrew J., *The Eisenhower Presidency Lessons for the Twenty-First Century,* 2015, Lexington Publishing, Washington, D.C.

Puryear Jr., Edgar F. 1971, 1992. *Nineteen Stars: a Study in Military Character and Leadership.* Novato, CA: Presidio Press. https://libquotes.com/dwight-d-eisenhower/quote/lbq1p3x.

Riley, Russell L., 1999, *The Presidency and the Politics of Racial Inequality Nation-Keeping from 1831 to 1965*. Columbia University Press: NY, NY

Ross Ryan, Halford (Ed.) The Inaugural Addresses of Twenthith-Century American Presidents, 1993, Prager Press, Westport, CT.

Roth, Ph.D., Henry J., ed. 2016. *All the Presidents' Memories: How They Reconstruct the Past, Manage the Present, and Shape the Future*. Vol. 1. Morrisville, NC: Lulu.com.

Sears, Alan, Craig Osten, and Ryan Cole. 2019. *The Soul of An American President: The Untold Story of Dwight D. Eisenhower's Faith*. Grand Rapids, MI: Baker Books.

Senate Committees on Armed Services and Foreign Relations, May 15, 1951.—Military Situation in the Far East, hearings, 82d Congress, 1st session, part 2, p. 732 (1951).

Simon, James F, 2018. *Eisenhower Vs Warren, The Battle for Civil Rights and Liberties,* NY, NY, Liveright Publishing Company.

Smith, Jean E. 2012. *Eisenhower: In War and Peace*. New York, NY: Random House Trade Paperbacks.

Social Networks and Archival Context. n.d. "1959 Steel Strike." 1959 Steel Strike. Accessed July 15, 2018. snacooperative.org.

Society for Personnel Administration. 1954. *The Federal Career Service: A Look Ahead*. Washington, D.C., USA: Society for Personnel Administration.

Stassen, Harold E., and Marshall Houts. 1990. *Eisenhower-Turning the World Towards Peace*. St. Paul, MN: Merrill/Magnus Publishing Corporation.

Stokesbury, James L. 1988. *A Short History of the Korean War*. New York, NY: William Morrow and Company, Inc.

Thomas, Evan. 2012. *Ike's Bluff: President Eisenhower's Secret Battle to Save the World*. New York, NY: Little, Brown, and Company.

Thompson, Kenneth W., ed. 1984. *The Eisenhower Presidency: Eleven Intimate Perspectives of Dwight D. Eisenhower*. Vol. III. Lanham, MD: University Press of America.

Thompson, Kenneth W. 1987. *Reevaluating Eisenhower: American Foreign Policy in the 1950s*. Edited by R. A. Melanson and D. A. Mayers. Urbana, Illinois: University of Illinois Press.

Tiffany, Paul A. 1988. *The Decline of American Steel*. New York, Oxford, NY: Oxford University Press.

Truman, Harry S. 1956. *Years of Trial and Hope*. New York, NY: Doubleday.

The United States, Department of State. 1990. *Foreign Relations of the United States*. Washington, D.C.: US Government Printing Office.

US National Security Council (NSC) and Dwight D. Eisenhower. 1953. "MINUTES OF DISCUSSION AT THE 150TH MEETING OF THE NATIONAL SECURITY COUNCIL, 18 JUNE 1953." Wilson Center Digital Archive. https://digitalarchive.wilsoncenter.org/document/111321.

US National Security Council (USC). 1953. "NSC 147." An *Analysis of Possible Courses of Action in Korea*. Washington, D.C.: Eisenhower Presidential Library.

United States Congress, Senate Committee on Foreign Relations, *Background Documents on Events Incident to the Summit Conference,* 1960, US Government Printing Office, Washington, D.C.

United States Congress, Senate Committee on Armed Services. *Francis Gary Powers Hearing Before the Committee on Armed Services, United States Senate, Eighty-seventh Congress, Second Session,* 1962, US Government Printing Office, Washington, D.C.

US White House. December 8, 1955. *Legislative Leadership Meeting.* Washington, D.C.: US White House.

US White House. March 9, 1956. *US Presidential Cabinet Meeting.* Washington, D.C.: US White House.

Walters, Vernon A. 2001. *The Mighty and the Meek: Dispatches from the Front Line of Diplomacy.* New York, NY: Little, Brown Book Group Limited.

DWIGHT D. EISENHOWER The American Presidents Series: The 34th President, 1953-1961

The American Presidents Tom Wicker; Arthur M. Schlesinger, Jr., General Editor, Times Books.

Weisbrode, Kenneth. 2018. *Eisenhower and the Art of Collaborative Leadership.* New York, NY: Anthem Press.

The White House. August 6, 1957. *Memorandum for the President.* Washington, D.C.: The White House.

Whittell, Giles. 2010. *Bridge of Spies.* New York, NY: Broadway Books.

Wise, David, and Thomas B. Ross. 1960. *The U-2 Affair.* New York, NY: Random House.

WordReference.com. 2019. "WordReference.com." WordReference.com. https://www.wordreference.com/definition/statesmanship#:~:text=states%E2%80%A2man%20(st%C4%81ts%E2%80%B2m%C9%99n,dealing%20with%20important%20public%20issues.

www.ourdocuments.gov. 1953. "Transcript of Armistice Agreement for the Restoration of the South Korean State." www.ourdocuments.gov. https://www.ourdocuments.gov/doc.php?flash=false&doc=85&page=transcript.

Lou Villaire

Index

A&E Television Networks, LLC: 29, 30, 201

Abel, Rudolf: 171

Acquaviva, Claudio: 1

African Americans: 20, 87-89, 94, 97, 103, 106, 111, 118-119, 183

Akka, Egyptian Ship: 75

Alexandria, Egypt: 62, 68

Ambrose, Stephen: 10, 146-152, 157, 159, 191-192, 201

America First Committee: 189

American Bar Association: 188

American Civil Liberties Union (ACLU): 93

American Presidency Project: 16-18, 34-35, 92, 94

Anderson, J. W: 92-93, 100

Aqaba, Gulf of, Egypt: 81

Arab Nationalism: 67, 82

Aralsk, Kazakhstan: 155

Arbenz, Jacobo - Guatemalan President: 19

Armas, Carlos Castillo: 19

Aswan Dam: 67-68, 78

Auerbach, Carl A: 110

Baier, Bret: 168, 202

Battle of Tel El Kebir: 63

Bay of Pigs, US Invasion of Cuba: 173

Beschloss, Michael R: 148, 151-154, 161-162, 164-167, 169-170, 172-174, 179

Ben-Gurion, Israeli Leader: 78

Blough, Roger M: 139, 141

Bodo, Norway: 155

Bradley, General Omar: 30, 39

British Petroleum (BP): 77

Brown vs Board of Education: 3, 91-92, 94, 101-104

Brownell, Herbert, US Attorney General: 56, 88-89, 91, 96-99, 104, 107-109, 183, 190

Buckley, William F. Jr.: 141

Byrd, Harry Senator of Virginia: 107

Byrnes, James F., Governor of South Carolina: 101

Cairo: 27, 67

Cairo Conference: 27

Camp David: 156, 166

Carnegie, Andrew: 123-124

Carnegie, Dale: 14, 202

Carey, Howard: 148

Caro, Robert A: 96, 103, 108-111, 117-118, 202

Central Powers: 63

Chiang Kai-shek: 24, 29, 37

Chinese-North Korean Command: 52

Chou En-lai: 149

Church, Frank, Senator of Idaho: 116

Churchill, Winston: 77

Cile, Ray: 147

Civil Rights Act of 1957 (CRA): 15, 20-21, 87-88, 95, 97-98, 100-103, 103-108, 110-111, 114-119, 183-184, 195

Civil Rights Movement: 7, 94, 195

Clark, General Mark: 39, 47-48, 50, 56

Cohen, Ben: 110

Cold War: 2, 18, 27-28, 167, 172, 174-175

Columbia Broadcasting System (CBS):10

Constantinople Convention of 1888: 62

Cow Palace, San Francisco, CA: 89

Crabtree, Steve: 23, 25, 52, 203

Crockett, David A: 190, 203

Cyclonite : 152

Dejean, Maurice : 73

Democratic National Convention: 16

Democratic Party: 16-17, 24, 34, 36, 88, 92, 99-100, 176, 202

Democratic People's Republic of Korea (DPRK): 28

Dependent Origination: 24-25, 178

Devine, Robert A: 61, 68-69 72, 79, 80, 82, 84, 168, 190, 203

Doran, Michael: 67, 203

Dulles, Allen: 162, 167, 175

Dulles, John Foster: 41, 46, 50, 68-71, 75-76, 82, 97, 149, 158, 199, 208

Eastern Buddhism: 24

Eden, Anthony, British Prime Minister: 69, 73-74, 77, 79-80, 83

Edwin, Ed: 46-47, 146, 202-203

Eisenhower Doctrine: 81-82, 84-85

Eisenhower, John: 46-47, 206

Eisenhower Peace: 24, 36

Ewald, Jr., William B: 206

Egypt: 6, 59, 61-62, 64-75, 77-78, 80-81, 83, 149, 183

Egyptian Free Officers Movement: 65

Egyptian Republic: 61, 65

Egyptian Revolution of 1952: 65

Farouk, King I: 65

Faubus, Orvil, Governor of Arkansas: 103

Fedayeen: 66, 81

Federal Bureau of Investigation (FBI): 91, 99, 141

Fisher, Roger, and Daniel Shapiro: 15, 206

Fisher, Roger, and Bill Ury: 11, 12, 207

Flemming, Arthur: 76

Formosa (Taiwan): 29, 149

Freedom House: 56

Fulbright, William Senator of Arkansas: 176, 177

Game of Bridge: 8, 9

Gary, Elbert Henry: 124

Gaza Strip: 71, 81

Generalissimo Chaing Kai-Shek: 24, 29, 37

Generalissimo Franco: 19

Geneva Peace Conference, 1955: 150

George, David Lloyd, British Prime Minister: 64

Getting to Yes: 11, 207

Gettysburg, US: 158

Glienicke Bridge, Berlin: 171

Goldberg, Arthur: 128, 129, 136, 207

Goldwater, Senator Barry of Arizona: 177

Goodpaster, General: 8, 152, 207

Greenstein, Fred I: 9, 207

Greenwich Mean Time (GMT): 155

Guatemala, Country of: 19, 82

Hagerty, James: 7, 112, 135-136, 206

Hall, Christopher G. 123, 206

Hazlett, Swede: 23, 204

Henderson, Loy: 73

Hermit Kingdom: 26

Herter, Christian, US Secretary of State: 159, 166-167

Hickenlooper, Bourke Senator of Iowa: 108

Hitchcock, William I: 77, 83, 97, 104, 108, 113, 116, 118, 153-154, 156, 161, 165, 174-177

Hoover, J. E., US FBI Director: 91, 207

Houts, Marshall: 40, 47-48, 210, 220

Hughes, Emmet J: 11, 72-74, 192, 207

Humes, J. C.: 187, 207

Hutchison, Van W: 207

Hussein, King of Jordan: 81, 82

Husseini, Hajj Amin al-: 67

Immerman, Richard H: 60, 82, 208

Inter-Continental Ballistic Missiles (ICBMs): 150, 156

International Monetary Fund (IMF): 79, 83

Iran, Country of: 18-19, 77, 82, 84

Iranian Prime Minister Mohammad Mosaddegh: 18

Japan–Korea Treaty of 1876: 26

Japan–Korea Treaty of 1910: 26

Jim Crow Laws: 87, 89

Johnson, Clarence L (Kelly): 146

Johnson, Lyndon Baines: 6, 81, 88, 100, 107, 116-117

Johnson, Olin Senator of Ohio: 108

Joseon, Kingdom of: 26

Kadesh Operation: 59

Kaiserslautern, West Germany: 148

Kefauver, Senator Estes: 17-18

Kennedy, John F: 6, 141, 150, 175, 177, 179, 186

Khrushchev, Nikita: 6, 31, 153, 155-160, 162-169, 1710174, 176-179, 186

Kim Il-sung: 28, 31, 46-47

King, Martin Luther, Jr.: 96, 98

Kirkuk, Iraq: 77

Kissinger, Henry: 30-33, 66, 68-70, 79-80, 82-83

Knowland, William Senator: 81, 93, 109-110, 112, 115

Korea: 4, 17, 23-29, 31-49, 51, 53-57, 121, 184

Korean Armistice12, 23-25, 33, 35-38, 40, 43-44, 46-55, 185

Korean Demilitarized Zone (DMZ): 23-24

Korean Peninsula: 24-27, 31, 37, 44

Korean People's Army: 53, 55

Korean War: 4, 7, 16, 20, 23-25, 27-28, 3043, 45-46, 49, 51-54, 56-57, 184, 195

Korda, Michael: 208

Kowert, Paul A: 191-193, 208

Kremlin, Hall of Columns: 169-170, 172-173

Land, Edwin H: 146-147

Leadership: 10, 13, 15, 23, 28, 37, 47, 56, 96, 99, 114, 117, 161, 177, 181, 188, 190, 191, 193

League of Nations: 64

Lippman, Walter: 161, 175

Little Rock Arkansas Central High School: 92, 103

Little Rock Nine: 106, 200

Lockheed, Corp: 146-148, 175

Lodge, Henry Cabot: 170

Lubyanka Prison in Moscow: 155

Luter, John: 49, 208

MacArthur, General Douglas: 24-25, 29-32, 36, 40, 47-48, 54, 56-57, 184

MacMillan, Harold, UK Chancellor of the Exchequer: 80, 83, 153, 164

Malinovsky, Rodion, Soviet Minister of Defense: 156, 165

Malta, Island of: 64

Manchuria: 29, 48

Mandate System: 64

Mao Zedong: 24, 28-29, 31, 46, 148

March Manifesto (Southern Manifesto), US Segregationist States, 1956: 104

Maritime Conference: 71

May Day: 152, 155

McDonald, David: 123, 128-130, 133-136, 138-140, 206

McElroy, Neil M., US Secretary of Defense: 151

McNamara, Robert US Secretary of Defense: 150

Medhurst, Martin J: 188, 208

Mennonite Church: 189

Mieczkowski, Yanek: 208

MiG Fighter Planes: 43

Military Armistice Commission (MAC): 53

Mississippi, State of: 18, 87, 96

Mitchell, James P., US Labor Secretary: 97, 132, 136-138, 140

Montgomery, General Bernard Law: 11

Morgan, Gerald D: 109, 123, 209

Morse, Wayne Senator of Oregon: 110

Moscow Conference: 27

Muhammad Ali Dynasty: 62

Murmansk, USSR: 155

MUSKETEER: 60

Nasser, Gamal Abdel: 6, 20, 59, 61, 65-70, 72-79, 82, 183

In Good Faith

National Archives: 29, 31, 45, 199, 209

National Aeronautics and Space Administration (NASA): 158

NATO Treaty: 2, 76

New Deal, FDR, US: 7, 88, 110

New York Herald Tribune: 161

Nichols, David A: 76, 88, 96, 106-109, 111-114, 116, 209

Nile River Valley: 68

Nixon, Richard M: 17-18, 51, 90, 109-110, 112, 132, 137-138, 141, 162, 175

North African Colonialism: 62

North Atlantic Treaty Organization (NATO): 2, 8, 10-11, 76, 183

North Korea: 23-26, 28-33, 36, 41-43, 45-56, 185

North Korean POWs: 52

Open Skies (US and USSR): 150

Operation Ajax: 77

Organization of Oil Exporting Countries (OPEC): 82

Ottoman Empire: 63-64

Pach, Jr., Chester J: 16, 209

Paris Peace Conference: 63-64, 163, 165, 176, 186

Paris Summit: 153, 162-169, 173, 175-176

Pasha, Isma'il: 62

Pasha, Sarwat, Egyptian Prime Minister: 64

Pasha, Tewfik: 62

Pearl Harbor: 169

People's Army of Mao Zedong: 24, 55, 198

People's Republic of China (PRC): 149

Peshawar, Pakistan: 155

Pineau, Christian: 73

Plessy vs Ferguson, US Supreme Court: 95, 101-102

Powell, Adam Clayton, Jr., Congressman from NY: 115

Powers, Francis Gary: 22, 145, 149-152, 154-156, 159, 162, 164, 169-171, 179, 185-186, 200, 212

Pravda: 173

Principled Negotiation: 11-13, 22, 118, 176

Purcell, Edward: 146-147

Puryear Jr., Edgar F: 1, 199, 209

Pyongyang: 31, 42-43

Rauh, Joe: 117

Republican National Convention, 1952 and 1956: 17, 189

Republican Party: 15-18, 2021, 24, 33-34, 36, 88-91, 95, 99, 111, 177, 189

Republican Party Platform: 33, 89, 90

Reston, James: 161

Rhee, Syngman: 6, 36, 39-41, 43, 50-51, 54-56

Riley, Russell L: 93, 210

River Brethren Church: 189

Robertson, Walter S. (Assist. Secretary of State): 51

Roosevelt, Franklin Delano: 15, 27, 88, 125

Ross, Thomas B: 159-160, 167-168, 171, 212

Roth, Ph.D., Henry J: 210

Russian POWs: 52

San Francisco Chronicle: 161

Saudi Arabia: 61, 83-84

Scott, Hugh Senator of PA: 161

Sears, Alan, Craig Osten, and Ryan Cole: 189, 210

Section Three, the CRA of 1957: 104, 110, 112

Semipalatinsk, USSR: 154

Seoul: 31

Shah, Mohammad Reza Shah of Iran: 18, 77

Sieker, Robert L: 148

Sinai: 72, 75, 78, 81, 149

Sixth US Fleet: 89

Smith, Jean E: 189-190, 210

Smith, General Walter Bedell: 192

Social Security: 7, 18

Society for Personnel Administration: 14

Sons of Islam: 66

Sons of Pharaoh: 66

South Korea (ROK): 6, 23-24, 26, 28-32, 36-42, 47-52, 54-57, 184-185

South Korean currency the Won: 54

South Vietnam: 18

Sparkman, Senator John: 16-17

St. Louis Post-Dispatch: 161

St. Louis, Missouri: 188

Stalin, Joseph: 28, 31, 40, 45-47, 52, 164

Stalingrad, USSR: 155, 164

Stassen, Harold E: 40, 47-48, 210

Steel Strike of 1959: 5, 21, 121-143, 185, 195

Stevenson, Adlai: 16-18, 92, 99-100, 184

Stokesbury, James L: 39, 43, 51, 53-53, 211

Stone, William, Governor of Ohio: 125

Suez Canal Company: 59-60, 62, 67-68, 71

Suez Crisis: 4, 20, 59-85, 149, 182-183, 195

Sverdlovsk, USSR: 145, 154-156

Taft-Hartley Labor Act (Labor Management Relations Act of 1947): 16, 110, 128-130, 132-133, 135-137, 142, 185

Taft, Robert Senator of Ohio: 18, 50, 189

Thomas, Evan: 9, 45-46, 159, 202, 206, 211, 212

Thompson, Kenneth W: 14, 56, 97, 181, 187-188, 190-191, 211

Thurman, Strom Senator of South Carolina: 36, 115

Tiffany, Paul A: 21, 124, 127-132, 139, 211

Till, Emmett: 96, 104, 113

Tripartite Aggression: 59, 72, 79

Truman, Harry S: 15-16, 23-25, 2834, 37, 56, 126, 128, 131, 184

Tuskegee Institute: 89

Tyuratam (now Kazakhstan): 154-156

U2 Incident: 5, 21-22, 145-180, 185-186, 195

UK: 18, 59, 62, 64, 69, 72-84, 183

UN Peacekeeping Force: 60, 78, 81

United Arab Emirates: 84

United Nations: 25, 28, 30, 38, 40-44, 47, 51-53, 55, 60, 71-72, 75, 78-79, 81, 183-185

United Nations Command: 28, 41, 43, 52-53

United States National Security Council (NSC): 29, 43-48, 50, 53, 56

United Steel Workers of America (USWA): 121, 122, 125, 136

US Army's 101st Airborne: 91, 103, 106

US Cape Canaveral: 155

US CIA: 19, 147-148, 151-152, 156-157, 162

US Civil War Reconstruction Era (1865–1877): 5, 101, 193

US Confederate States: 101

US GDP: 7, 55

US House of Representatives: 93, 99, 112, 135

US Interstate Highway System: 3

US Joint Chiefs of Staff: 30, 41, 48, 151-152, 184

US Justice Dept, Civil Rights Commission: 90, 92-94, 100, 105, 111

US Kiwanis' Clubs: 24, 36

US Mutual Security Agency: 47-48

US Reconstruction States: 89

In Good Faith

US Steel Corporation (USS): 6, 121-123, 126, 141

US Steel Industry: 5, 21, 121, 123-125, 127, 141, 185

US Strategic Air Command (S.A.C.): 148

US Supreme Court: 90-92, 94-96, 99, 101-104, 117, 126, 129, 134, 136, 183

USSR: 26-32, 36, 41, 43, 46, 52, 55, 61, 68-70, 73, 75, 80, 82, 84, 145-180, 183, 186

Urabi, Ahmad: 62

Urabi, Ahmed: 63

Wafd Party: 63

Walters, Vernon A: 10-11, 212

Washington Post: 161

Washington, Val: 109, 113

Weisbrode, Kenneth: 10, 13, 14

Whittell, Giles: 162, 170-171, 212

Whitman, Ann: 96, 161, 167

Whitney, Catherine: 168, 202

Wiesbaden, Germany: 146

Wilkins, Roy: 116

Wingate, Sir Reginald, British High Commissioner: 63

Wise, David: 156, 159-160, 167-168, 171, 212

231

WWI: 18, 64-65

WWII: 3, 11, 14, 18, 22, 26-28, 35, 40, 46, 52, 65, 125-126, 164, 177, 192

WWII Pax Americana: 2

Yalta Conference: 27

Yalu River: 43, 48

Yekaterinburg, Kirov: 154-156

Yi Seonggye. Korean Dynasties: 26

Zaghlul, Saad: 63-64

Zhukov, General Georgy: 164

About the Author

Dr. Lou Villaire is a former lecturer at Colorado Mesa University (CMU) in Grand Junction, CO. At CMU, Dr. Villaire taught undergraduate courses in American Government, Public Policy, and Public Administration. Dr. Villaire has taught undergraduates in American Studies for almost two decades. Dr. Villaire's undergraduate students have taught him that the story of American History is relevant for individuals today, demonstrated by their personal experiences as Americans.

Dr. Villaire earned a BA in English and Environmental Studies from Western Michigan University and an MA in Environmental Policy from the University of Illinois, Chicago. Dr. Villaire holds a doctorate in Political Science from Northern Illinois University. He is co-owner of a solar energy company in Western Colorado.

Lou Villaire

Endorsement for *In Good Faith*

In Good Faith is a real addition to the tradition of political biographies. It offers a roadmap into the mind of President Eisenhower. For Ike, the secret to a great negotiator was to know the mind of those in the negotiations. To that end, this work offers a key to the mind of the master negotiator during this critical period of US history. It belongs in the collection of anyone seriously trying to understand the early days of the cold war, the civil rights movement, and the rapid growth in American prosperity during the 1950s."

Tim Casey, PhD
Professor of Political Science, Colorado Mesa University

For decades Dwight Eisenhower was considered a mediocre president. Lou Villaire has vividly detailed and cogently written about Ike's strengths and weaknesses through several complex foreign and domestic events, and why he deserves to be considered one of the best presidents.

Dr. Irwin Gellman
Author - *The President and the Apprentice: Dwight Eisenhower and Richard Nixon 1952-1961*

This fascinating study brings the Eisenhower era and Ike to life. From the Korean War, Suez crisis, and Civil Rights Act to the steel strike and U2 spy plane incident, the author adopts a unique, revealing focus on President Eisenhower's negotiation skills. Dr. Villaire convincingly argues that Ike's unusual ability to negotiate significantly contributed to his political and policy successes. The author also creatively positions his account as a leadership and management training guide. Indeed, you will learn much about how to negotiate better from this president."

Brendon Swedlow, PhD, JD
Professor, Department of Political Science
Northern Illinois University

Made in United States
North Haven, CT
16 April 2022